THE TIES THAT BIND US

THE TIES THAT BIND US

Elizabeth D Moss

ATHENA PRESS
LONDON

ISBN 1 84401 709 5

First Published 2006 by
ATHENA PRESS
Queen's House, 2 Holly Road
Twickenham TW1 4EG
United Kingdom

Printed for Athena Press

I

The year was 1947 and it was in the month of February. It was a bleak and dismal outlook, weather-wise. The snow was about two feet in height already and it was still falling at a steady rate. It was one of the worst years we had ever had as regards the weather, or so I was told many years later.

It was early evening and panic ran through the one-up, one-down cottage that my future parents rented. The panic came from my father-to-be and the reason for that panic was the fact that my mother had had to send for him from the public house and there was still an hour's drinking time left. Her labour pains had started one hour earlier and she had no way of getting to the nursing home without my father's help.

My father was never a patient man at the best of times and lived for the booze and his drinking friends. Everything else came second to him, including his family. He was excessively violent after his drinking sprees and he certainly was not in the best of moods, having been brought from the pub to see to my mother.

My father had been in the Royal Air Force up until two years before. He now worked as a builders' labourer. He was a slim-built man then, not very tall, perhaps about 5′3″. He was quite popular in the small village where we lived. The reason for this was that no one really knew him except my mother and the next-door neighbours. Only they could hear my mother's cries when he beat her up after he came home drunk.

Mother was a very small-built woman, only about five feet tall and very slender, she was a very attractive lady. The people that knew about my father beating her could never understand why she married him, but he was never violent until they got married. When she first met my father Mother had been engaged to a Canadian officer and my grandparents were very much against the match. A week before the marriage they threw my mother out. Perhaps they hoped it would bring her to her senses and she would not go through with the wedding.

My mother was booked into a private nursing home for my birth, perhaps because she always insisted that she was carrying twins even though the doctor said she was only having one child.

Father finally went to see if he could get transport to take my mother to the nursing home, as it was two miles down the road in the nearest town. I dare say that if it hadn't been such a treacherous night and she had not been so far advanced in her labour he would have made her walk to the nursing home.

There were problems on the phone: it seemed that because it was such a rotten night the taxi driver was reluctant to turn up. Father had to give him double fare before he would agree to come out. This upset my father even more, it meant that now he had even less money for the pub, so my mother got more verbal abuse when he came back from the phone. He would probably have struck her, had she not been going on to the nursing home. However, his parting words to her just as the taxi arrived were: 'I hope you die and those two bastards with you' – charming man.

Father now had to deal with my older brother who had been sleeping upstairs while my mother had been getting ready to leave. Father had to eat humble pie and see if my grandmother would have him while mother was away.

My grandparents lived just up the street from our house, in fact it was through them that my parents got their house, as my grandfather was in the building trade and knew an awful lot of people. When the house became empty he knew the man it belonged to and he arranged for my parents to rent it.

It was only after my older brother had been born that my grandparents decided to accept my father. I suppose the fact that it was their first grandchild had a lot to do with their decision. You see, my mother was their only child so they had a lot to lose if they didn't accept my father.

My father went up to the pub with my brother Fred, who was nearly two years old to see if my grandmother would look after him. The reason he went up to the pub with Fred was because my grandparents had tenancy of the local public house; Grandmother ran the pub during the day as Granddad ran his building business with the help of my father whom he employed in those days.

My grandmother was quite happy that my mother had finally gone into labour at long last and said she would have my brother until my mam came home. She was not very happy, however, about the fact that she had lost her helper. My mother had to go each morning to help scrub the place out and wash the glasses and things ready for the dinnertime opening; she then had to go back in the evening and help with the cooking and serving of drinks at the bar. They had a lot of trade in those days as the buses would pull in and expect meals or snacks to be served. My grandmother was not a lazy woman, far from it, but my mother came a lot cheaper than one of the local woman in the village. Still, my gran would have to put up with it till mother came home.

In the meantime, Mother was laid in a small room at the nursing home awaiting my arrival. The staff there consisted of one midwife and one nurse. The midwife ran the establishment and left it until the last possible moment before she called the doctor in. So my poor, patient mother lay in the small side room until the pain got too much for her and she summoned the midwife, who, in turn, after checking my mother, decided that it was time to call in the doctor.

The doctor had known my mother for a number of years and knew the kind of life that she had with my father, so he was very sympathetic, a good doctor for my mother to be under.

She told the doctor that there were two babies, but he would not have that at all. It was not that he was inadequate; it was just the fact that in those days they had no such things as scanners or modern technology.

My arrival into the big bad world had at last arrived, they told my mother she had a little girl and my mother informed them that there was another one about to make its arrival into the world.

I was bundled out of the way into a side room where the midwife placed me into a cot and put a hot-water bottle in with me while she went back to help the doctor with the delivery of the second child.

You can imagine my mother's delight at the thought of twins, even though she was in a lot of pain. Still it was not to be, the other child arrived dead, or so they informed my mother. She still insists to this very day that my sister was very much alive; she said she felt her move against her leg as she made her entrance into the world.

I guess no one will ever know.

The attitude in 1947 was to pacify the patient, who was not allowed to have an opinion. My little sister was thrown into a bucket under the delivery table until they cleaned my mother up. After all, she was dead so could be seen to later.

My mother was cleaned up and settled into her little room, after all this is what my parents paid for. Imagine my mother's feelings at this time, she had just lost one child and had not as yet seen me and here she was laid in a little room, isolated, wondering how I was and possibly how my father would be when she finally got to see him. After all they didn't part on very good terms.

While all this had been going on, I had been left in a cot with my hot-water bottle and no supervision. I had no nappy on and while I laid there I had scalded myself. My urine had hit the hot water bottle, or so I was later informed by my mother, and had somehow scalded me. I don't even understand it to this day; all I really know is that the scars I still bear prove that something went wrong many years ago.

Panic now ran riot in the nursing home, after all you don't pay fees to lose one child and have another one very near to death's door. The major decision now was how to inform my poor mother about my condition and get her permission to transfer me immediately to the nearest large hospital that could deal with first-degree burns on a small child.

My mother was totally horrified, but at that stage in her life she was a very quiet woman; she didn't know how to deal with the situation, so she had to leave everything in the doctor's hands.

They put me into the nearest hospital that could deal with major burns and that was only because they had just employed a big specialist within the last two days. In that much I suppose my parents were lucky.

My father now had to be contacted and informed about the whole situation so the nurse phoned the pub. They told him nothing over the phone except for the fact that my mother had given birth and was OK. They suggested he came down to the hospital.

Father came rushing down to the nursing home in a worried state of mind and not exactly cool, calm and collected.

He was probably worried that he'd caused some reaction in my mother with his behaviour before she went into the nursing home. When he finally found out what had happened to me through the nurse's neglect, and the fact that he was the father of identical twins, or rather had been, he was like a man demented.

His first thought, believe it or not, was to rush into the side room to see how my mother was feeling. As you can guess she was not a very happy woman at all; well, who would be under the circumstances? She informed him where I was and asked him to come through to see the specialist to find out exactly what my condition was and how badly I was scalded. My father had to remind my mother about the bad weather conditions and the fact that the hospital was situated some twelve miles away.

Father stayed with my mother as long as he possibly could, but had to go home to tell my grandparents what had happened. There was also my brother to consider, he had been left in the care of my grandparents, but they had the pub to run. When he finally left my mother she was sleeping after her ordeal. Before she dropped off he promised her he would return first thing in the morning.

My father arrived back at the pub about half an hour after leaving the nursing home, by which time he was very wet, tired and very depressed. My grandparents at this time were run off their feet in the pub, as it was Saturday night. Two bus-loads full of people had just arrived and were demanding cooked meal, and, due to the fact that they had no one to help them, as my mother was not available, they could not really pay my father much attention. However, he managed to enquire of them if my brother could stay at the pub for the rest of the evening, seeing that he was now fast asleep in his cot upstairs. In between all the rushing around looking after their customers my grandparents said he could stay.

My father sat very quietly in a corner nursing his pint of beer and not saying anything to anyone at all. This was very unusual for him he was usually the life and soul of the pub. I suppose he was just waiting until the pub closed so he could inform my grandparents about their new granddaughter and where I was, plus the condition I was in.

He managed a game of darts with some of the local lads and, on them inquiring about my mother's whereabouts, just told them she had gone into labour earlier on this evening and he was still waiting to find out the results. After all, he couldn't tell them anything else in case it got back to my grandparents before he'd informed them.

Closing hour was fast approaching, the buses had departed and it was mainly only the few regulars that were left to kick out. Grandfather started clearing the tables of all the empty glasses and he could not believe it when my father offered to help with the washing up in the back kitchen. Possibly that was what alerted him to the fact that something was not as it should be. They closed the pub doors on time that night.

My grandparents left the clearing up in the bar to wait till morning and went through into their living quarters. By this time my grandmother was very worried. How on earth could my father tell them that their one and only daughter had given birth to twins, and one had died while the other one was lying in the hospital in very critical condition?

How did my grandparents react? Grandmother was bloody furious and wanted to go down to the nursing home right there and then; it took my grandfather quite a time to calm her down. He said there was no chance of them getting the car out at this time of the night and there was nothing they could do even if they did go to the nursing home. They all finally retired after deciding what they were going to do tomorrow. My grandmother was the logical one. She never let emotions interfere with her decisions, so she decided to see how I was the next morning and then go and talk to my mother.

The visit had to be done very early because my grandparents still had the pub to open up and run for the dinner time. At least it was Sunday, so the opening hours were very much shorter than during the week. On their visit to the hospital, they found me on a drip-feed and the surgeon waiting for permission to operate on me. They gave him written consent there and then, because he told them that my chance of survival until morning would be nil without the first of many operations.

They all left the hospital in very poor spirits, all, that is, except my grandmother who I have been told was furious. She made my grandfather drive straight to the nursing home while she was still in that frame of mind. On their arrival at the home my father went straight to my mother's room to see how she was feeling after her night's sleep. She was still very upset and worried: upset over the loss of one daughter and worried about me. My father told her that the family had all been to the hospital and that I was having an operation later on that day; to give him his due he was really trying to put her mind at rest.

Next my grandfather walked into the room. He was a great guy, six feet two inches in stature and walked very straight and upright. Possibly this was because he'd been a captain in the army early on in his life, which was where he met and married my grandmother. Grandfather was always a great comforter to my mother but he never treated her with kid gloves or hid anything from her. So, in his opinion, there was no reason why he should start now. He told her that things didn't look too good for me at the moment and she had better prepare herself for the loss of another daughter. He said that if I survived it would be a miracle in his opinion.

My grandmother then showed her face. She had been with the midwife trying to get to the truth of what had happened the night I was brought into the world. She was not very satisfied with the midwife's explanation of my being put out of the way while they dealt with my mother.

She thought that a solicitor should be consulted first thing tomorrow. As far as she was concerned there had been neglect on the part of the midwife as regarded my welfare.

My mother pointed out the fact that there was no money to pay for such things as solicitors. It had to be pointed out to my mother, in turn, that if it turned out to be a case of neglect as my grandmother suspected, there wouldn't be a penny to pay, as the midwife would have to pay all the solicitor's fees. In the year of 1947, all the medical bills had to be paid for by someone and if it turned out that it was a case of neglect, as my grandmother suspected, then the midwife would have bandages and creams to pay for as well. It was a good job that you didn't have to pay for the operations too.

The next day my grandfather drove my father to work and left him to carry on with the job they were doing at that particular time. He had booked an appointment to see the solicitor about my medical bills and the treatment I was undergoing. The main thing as far as my grandfather was concerned was to put my mother's mind at rest about the financial aspect, not so much as regards me, because he thought my chances of survival were nil.

After great discussions with the legal people, the conclusion seemed to be that there was a great deal of neglect on behalf of the midwife and she would be responsible for payment of any medical treatment I had to receive, but that it would eventually lead to a court case. Grandfather, satisfied with that for the present, then proceeded to the nursing home to visit my mother for a while and to inform her about the visit to the solicitor and how things were progressing.

Now mother at this time was getting very frustrated being stuck in bed and not even having a child there with her. She was also fretting over my brother as this was the first time she had ever left him with anyone. My mother was a very determined lady and was not one for lying in bed, regardless of the fact that she had just gone through a very difficult labour. The only time I guess she would ever stay laid up in bed would be a time when she didn't have the strength to get up and fight. She wanted to go home, see my brother and see me – in that order.

Grandfather persuaded her to stay where she was for the present time, telling her there was nothing she could do if she went home so she was much better off staying where she was.

Mother had a great respect for my grandfather and, even though she was now a grown-up, married woman with a family of her own, she would never dream of disobeying him. The only time she had ever disobeyed him was when she married my father, and that resulted in much sorrow.

Grandmother was hard at work at the pub and finding it very difficult without my mother there to help her, and even worse having little Frederick to look after. After the dinnertime opening, she got a taxi down to the nursing home to visit with my mother for a while. She couldn't stop for too long as she had the pub to reopen at night time again and also my grandfather's dinner to cook. She was also very reluctantly feeding my father. She was very sharp-tongued women, but she did believe in a man having a good meal after a hard day's work.

Father came in, had his meal, and went down to see my mother before opening time, when he would then spend the rest of his evening in the pub, no doubt getting all the sympathy of the locals who both liked and respected my mother. On his visit to my mother she told him arrangements had to be made to bury my twin sister. In 1947, or so I was told, my sister could not have a proper funeral, owing to the fact that she had not been baptised. The church would not let her be buried inside the churchyard so she had to be buried outside the churchyard. This was left for my father to sort out.

My mother told my father she would be home the next day anyway, where at least she could be of some use rather than stuck in the nursing home. Father didn't try to talk her out of it, after all, he would get his home life back again and wouldn't have to put up with my grandmother nagging at him. I, by this time, had undergone my first operation and seemed to be doing all right, not that I knew very much about it.

Father arranged for the undertaker to build him a small coffin for my sister, which he would pick up next day. He also arranged with a friend to help him dig a grave just outside the churchyard wall under a big old oak tree where they planned to bury my little sister.

The next day mother got a taxi home and took my brother back home with her. He was very pleased to see her, as he could not understand where she had gone away in the first place. Perhaps if she could have shown him his new sister it would have been easier for both of them.

After work my father biked down to the undertakers to collect my little sister's coffin and then on to the nursing home to get her body. He then had to tuck the little coffin under his arm and bike back up to the churchyard where he had arranged to meet his friend for the burial. On his way home with the box under his arm, he, by mistake, let it slant down and the tiny body slid in the box. I write about this because later on in my life mother told me of this incident and said that it affected my father for years to come.

The years went by and nothing much altered. Mother still worked herself into the ground at my grandparents' public house; Father still drank all the money. These days, however, he often did his drinking away from home, down in the little town were I was born. He had got to know a whole lot of new people, all like himself, hardened drinkers. Mother still had to put up with the beatings and the verbal abuse. How she ever survived I for one will never know.

II

Most of my early childhood was spent in the local hospital having one operation after another. I came home to be with my family at least six months out of every year.

When I was four years old I attended the village school along with my brother. I have no recollection of my early school days whatsoever. In fact, about the first ten years of my life are pretty blank spaces to me. I often wonder now in the later years of my life if something dramatic happened to me to blank out my early childhood years.

My start at school only lasted five months and then, much to my parents surprise, they got an offer from the local council of a three-bedroom house. The council had just built an estate in the small village of Tow, about a mile outside of the town where I was born. Mother was over the moon about it and could hardly wait for my father to get home from work to tell him about it. We had all lived in the cottage for years and there were only two rooms altogether, one which we all shared – my brother and I in one bed and my parents in another bed. So in the new house it would be great for all of us. It meant my brother could have a room of his own, and I could have my own room – trust us kids not to worry about furniture or logical things like that.

Would you believe it, father came home and, after his meal, Mother told him about the offer. He was delighted about it, perhaps due to the fact that he would be away from my grandparents and nearer his newfound friends.

They accepted the house and arranged to see it at the weekend when my father was not at work. It turned out to be the first one in a block of twenty-five to be completed; it was great, two big bedrooms and one smaller one, a bathroom upstairs. We had never used a bathroom before, it was always the tin bath in front of the fire in the cottage. There were two toilets, one upstairs and one downstairs, the downstairs one was situated in a back porch next to a big washhouse where mother could do all her washing, and then there was the coalhouse – luxury. There was the kitchen-cum-dining-room that was all one big room and then there was a separate room which was kept as the best room and used for special occasions only. To us it was a dream house after the cottage.

Grandfather helped us to move a week later as he had his wagon that he used for work. There wasn't really that much to move and it all seemed a bit lost in that great big house. I still shared a room with my brother, as we only had the one bed at present. Mother showed me which room I was going to have and promised me she would have it done as soon as possible for me. A big promise for her, seeing as father was never keen to part with his money at the best of times.

Thinking back over my life now, I realise what a brilliant mother she was in the way that she kept the home going. Without her there would never have been a home. She was the only person I knew that could make a meal out of next to nothing.

Mother had now lost her small but useful income because of the move so she had to set about finding a job as soon as she possibly could. Over the last four years she had managed to save some money, god knows how. That went on furniture for the kitchen-cum-dining-room, as we always called it. Being a very determined lady she soon found a job with a farmer doing all kinds of field work: potato picking, harvesting, hedging, gardening. In fact, she turned her hand to anything that was to be done around the place.

Her day started around five in the morning when she arose and cleaned the house, prepared the evening meal, laid the fire and saw to our breakfasts and all our needs before she set off to work. She left us about an hour before school, with strict instructions to behave ourselves. We didn't dare do otherwise, at least I didn't.

She was home about an hour after we returned from school. Yes, these days it would be illegal to do what she did, but the laws were not so severe back then. No one cared about unsupervised children as they do now.

We carried on with our schooling while mother worked herself stupid to build up our home. She was so house-proud that if we even put our hands on the furniture it would mean a clip around the earhole.

I still spent a lot of my time in hospital and every time my parents came to visit me it was with a big present. They seemed to think it made up for my loss of time spent with them. I had everything any girl could ever want, a sewing machine that sewed, a cooker that cooked, dolls that walked, a doll's pram, a doll's house, a swing in the garden – you name it, I had it. Yet they never meant a thing to me. Ungrateful? No. It's just that I would have traded them all for a cuddle on my mother's knee.

Mother was never a very demonstrative woman and showed very little affection throughout our lives. I never realised how important this was to me until later on in my life. I suppose she brought us up the only way that she knew how. We all make mistakes in the upbringing of our children and none of us realise until after the event.

The move to the new house certainly didn't alter my father at all, if anything he was worse than before, as he now had all his new friends. In fact since we had moved, one of his friends had moved into a new house across the road. He was a married man with five children. At that time the only difference between our family and his was the fact that my mother was a very clean, house-proud women, whereas his wife didn't really bother about her house or the state of her children. They always had shaven hair because of the nits and they spent most of their time sitting on the kerb outside the house with a crust of bread in their little grubby hands. Mother wouldn't let us anywhere near them.

The worst times would be the weekends, particularly Saturday nights. We used to stay awake on a Saturday night until father had come in from his drinking spree. I don't know what we thought we could do when he beat Mother up, but perhaps we thought we were safer awake then asleep. At least we could escape if we were awake. Father had usually been drinking all day and would only come home to eat. If his meal was not on the table or not to his liking when he came in, it would end up on the ceiling; the table and chairs would most likely follow. After that Mother would get a good hiding because things were not right for him.

He would then take himself off to bed and mother would be expected to follow as if nothing had ever happened, after all, she was his wife and he would probably want his rights. He would have a couple of hours sleep and then get up and return to the pub with his friends, where he would drink himself into a stupor and come home about midnight. Then more than likely he would give my mother a bit more grief – it would depend on whether he had been upset while at the pub. Like all wife-beaters he was a coward outside the home.

Father wasn't always the same, sometimes he could be nice and sometimes quite funny, it all depended on how much he'd had to drink.

I was only six years old and had already undergone five operations and had also survived pneumonia twice, bronchitis and – the worst of the lot – meningitis. It's small wonder the doctors informed my parents that if I lived to be seven it would be a miracle.

Well, I'm still here to tell my story.

It was nearly Christmas, which was always great, as every year we would travel down south to visit my father's younger sister and her husband. She loved us to bits. She always used to call us her kids and spoilt us something rotten. She was the manageress of a local cooperative store, so money was never a problem to her. My uncle was a coal miner in a local mine. They owned their own house and we used to stay there with them for a whole week. So in a funny kind of way we had two Christmas's – one down south with them and another one when we returned home with my parents.

I absolutely adored my aunt, in fact, if it boiled down to it I thought more of her than I did of my own mother, perhaps it was due to this fact that she gave me plenty of cuddles and all the affection that my mother didn't seem to give me.

But, the holiday soon went and we would return back to normal life, well, normal to us.

Mother had built up a lovely home. There was a bedroom suite in my room and the same in my brother's. The front room – as we called it – was like a palace, not a thing out of place. We were not allowed to go in there, in fact the only time it was used was on special occasions such as Christmas or when we had visitors, which was not very often. It was a beautiful home, but it wasn't a *real* home because we could never be in there and we were scared stiff of making a mess with anything.

The years rolled by, I always had the best of everything as regards clothes and shoes. There is one occasion that I remember. Mother had just bought me a new dress and coat and I was packed off to Sunday school. The only problem was that I never went to Sunday school, but spent my collection money on sweets and took myself down to the fields to play by the waterside. It didn't matter to me that there was no one else there as I preferred my own company most of the time. I had spent so much time in hospital that I had never been able to make friends. Well, back to the fact that I should have been at Sunday school and had never been anywhere near the church. I had no watch on so I had no idea what time it was and I was too busy having a good time in the fields that I didn't really care. Before I knew it, it had started to get dark and I suddenly realised I could not possibly return home as my mother would now know for certain I had not been going to Sunday school. Talk about being scared stiff. I was too scared to go home because I knew there would be hell to pay for what I had done and I was scared of the fields as it was now getting dark. The fields no longer held the attraction they had before, in fact now they looked quite menacing, with shadows and images behind every tree and bush.

Where to go and what to do, that was the question; the trouble was, where was the answer? I did not know, but as all these thoughts were travelling round in my head the answer was walking down the road in the form of my mother. Was she annoyed! She had our little dog with her, but he was not on the lead as normal, I soon found out why. Although I tried to explain why I had not do as I was told, it was to no avail. To make matters worse, I had climbed over fences during my time out and my new dress and coat had a big rip in them.

Mother took that dog lead and she belted me all the way home with it. On our arrival home I was promptly bathed and sent to bed with nothing to eat. I can tell you I never pulled that stunt again.

I was by now nine years old and came home from school as usual, but today was different. My mother was at home when I came in which I found to be very nice. She seemed in an excellent mood and not rushing round like she usually was, but sitting down having a cup of tea. My brother had not yet arrived home from school so there was only my mother and myself in the house. She chatted away to me about school and how I liked it and what I had been doing at school today. *It's not normal*, I thought, *something's going on, that's for sure*. In came my brother. He wasn't very pleased to see my mother at home, it meant he couldn't bully me tonight and do everything he wanted to do.

My mother got up to start doing the dinner ready for my father when he came home, which would be in about an hour's time providing he did not call at the pub. After changing from our school clothes so we could go out into the garden, Mother told us we had to be back in the house when our father came home as she had something important to tell us all.

Now what? Were we leaving my father? Were we leaving the area? What was going on? My brother and I were baffled, it was not very often that we had family meetings.

Father came home on time, which made a nice change – it seemed like everything was running smoothly for once and that would make Mother very happy. Mother shouted us in after father had arrived home and said it was teatime. *This is a one-off*, I thought as we all sat around the table together. *It's nice, why can't we be like this all the time?* Some hope.

After we had finished our meal, Mother cleared the table and made a pot of tea. As we all sat around the table she said she would now tell us all what we were all entitled to know as it would concern us all in the long term. She said she had been to the doctors today and he had told her there was going to be another addition to the family, we would have another brother or sister in our home. Father seemed over the moon about it and actually invited my mother out with him for a drink to celebrate the fact that he was going to be a father again.

My brother seemed unconcerned about it all and just wanted to go back out and play with his friends; Mother said he could go, but he had to be back by suppertime. When I asked if I could go back out she said that she needed to talk to me. Now what had I done wrong? Probably nothing, but that seemed to be the way my life went – I always seemed to be in bother about the most little things.

As my mother had refused my father's invitation to go out he had gone upstairs to have a soak in the bath before he went out with his friends. Mother said that now that she was going to have a baby she would expect me to help her all I could with the household chores. There was no mention of my brother helping her out at all. I didn't mind as it would be quite exciting to have a baby in the house. Personally I couldn't wait. When I went to school the next day I told everyone that we were having a new baby in our house and they all seemed as happy as me about the arrival.

My mother still kept on working. I thought that she would have stopped at home now that she was having a baby – the things that you think when you are young! Well, at least she would have to stop working once the baby arrived so that she could look after it.

My father seemed to have settled down since we had found out that there was to be a new baby in the house. I wondered how long that would last. He was even being generous with his wages and my mother and he seemed quite happy these days. Perhaps it was the pregnancy sheltering her? Things seemed to settle into a pretty quiet routine for a short while. Maybe it was going to be different with my father now there was a new addition arriving. I wish I could say that he parted with some more money for the pram and things, but I guess that would have been too much to ask, after all his beer money couldn't take a drop, which explained why mother was still working.

It must have been hard, after all she was doing a man's job on a farm. My mother had two bosses – brothers with two different farms. They were very good to her, allowing her to work the hours that fitted in with family commitments. No one actually knew what a bastard my father was; they all thought he was a lovely man, the life and soul of the party.

Anyway mother bought a beautiful pram, the best there was in the shop. It had a false bottom to put all your shopping under the baby, I couldn't hardly see over the handle to look into it.

Myself, well, I had just started a new school two-and-a-half miles from home. A long walk each morning and Mother made me come home at lunchtime so I could do jobs before returning to school. The amount of times I got into trouble at school for returning late from lunch is unbelievable, but I was too scared of Mother to defy her or tell the teachers the truth so they thought I was a defiant child. I couldn't win really.

I remember one occasion at lunchtime, Mother said I had to go to the town a mile away for the shopping. I knew I couldn't possibly do it so I pleaded with her to let me go after school, but no joy. So, what I did was, I set off with a plan to steal a bike from the pub yard and put it back on my return. I knew it was wrong, but I thought it would cut down on the time it took me to get to town and back and Mother would get her shopping and be pleased and I might get back to school on time.

It worked, I got back to school just as everyone was lining up to go in and no one was any the wiser. I got home at teatime, ate and then was allowed to go out and play after I'd done my chores, I must have pleased her. We drew a hopscotch on the road in the street; the neighbours didn't like it very much and we were usually given a bucket of water to scrub it off after, but it was fun playing at the time. Some nights we would go round and torment the old people who lived round the corner, one old chap was not quite right and we used to really wind him up. If Mother had ever known there would have been hell to pay but that was something she never found out.

Well, when it was time to go in while Mother was still in a good mood. My elder brother always got extra time out, which I thought was unfair, but there was nothing I could do about it. I got washed ready for bed while Mother was doing supper – one thing I will always say about her is that we never went hungry. I suppose because the kids over the way used to sit on the kerb with nothing but a slice of bread. Sometimes they didn't even have any socks on.

I was just eating my supper and there was a knock on the door. Who should it be, but the police? Big Brother must have been watching, I thought, as I had forgotten the bike incident. When they told my mother that I had stolen a bike at lunchtime, I knew that I was in big trouble. It was just a telling off from the police I had returned the bike, but when they had gone, out came the stick which mother kept in the corner.

Funny, I can never remember my brother getting hit with it.

I begged her not to hit me and promised that I would never do anything like that again, but she wouldn't listen. It wouldn't have been too bad if she only gave me a couple of whacks, but she never seemed to know when to stop. If I fell on the floor hoping to escape the stick, she would pull me back up by my hair. *Why does she hate me so much?* I kept asking myself. I cried myself to sleep that night for sure.

Never mind, I thought, *about three months to go and there would be a new baby in the house and perhaps it would change things a bit.*

Don't take me wrong, I loved my mother to bits, but I never thought she loved me. She did all the right things as regards feeding and washing us. What I hated was that she was rough and if I cried because she had got soap in my eyes I would get the whole bar shoved in my mouth – and in those days it was usually a big bar of carbolic and it stung. Our beds were always lovely and clean with nice white sheets. I always remember that once a week on bath nights nails were cut, ears cleaned out and nice fresh nightclothes off to a lovely fresh bed.

Father was still drinking, but at least was not hitting Mother, just shouting a lot. One Sunday, because she had not sugared his cup of tea, he threw the tea at her and then the table went flying and a lot of other things too, he then went up to bed before his night-time binge. Mother was in tears, after all her house was her pride and joy. I helped her clean it up and she gave me some money for some sweets. I went up to the little sweet shop, which was quite far, nearly up in the town, but it was a nice little shop, full of lovely things for children, it was so hard to decide.

Why I did what I did I will never know. Perhaps I wanted to hurt someone because I was always getting hurt, who knows. There were two children at the sweet shop and on the way home I bumped into them. We walked so far home together then they had to go another way. So what did I do? I hit them, took their sweets and sent them home crying. It made me feel really good, perhaps I had an evil streak in me.

I used to do things like that most of the time, but it was usually after Mother had beaten me that I would go out and beat someone up in return. I remember one boy in particular who had only had one arm and I guess he was an easy target for me. I don't know why I did it but it was like a vicious circle, Mother would beat me and I would go out and beat someone, then their mother would come round to our house and tell my mother and I would get beaten again. None of it made any sense really.

Life went on pretty much as usual with Mother leaving very early for work and my brother and I seeing ourselves off to school. He was at the new big school just round the corner from were we lived, lucky devil. But I would go there in a year's time.

It would soon be Christmas again. It wouldn't be the same though as we were not going to my auntie's down south. I didn't know if I would enjoy it as much without her. Mother had to finish work at Christmas because the baby would be here shortly after. Auntie sent a big parcel up for us and when I opened all my presents she had sent all my favourite books, I loved books and reading at night after I'd gone to bed. I had to be sneaky though as Mother would make me turn the light off when I went to bed. I hated turning the light off as I was very frightened of the dark, I would always look under my bed and in my wardrobe then dive into bed and pull the covers over my head. I remember a time when I went to sleep with the light on and got into bother the next morning.

Mother used to send me to the fish shop at odd times and I remember one time in particular she sent me. The road to the fish shop was very dark and spooky and you had to pass this old caravan that stood in a field. The children always said it was haunted. I would always run past it looking back all the time as I ran past.

On my way back this particular evening the bushes started to shake and there were strange noises coming from somewhere. I just dropped the fish and chips and ran home as fast as I could go. Mother was really annoyed then I went in crying without the tea and told me I had to go back out again. Just then my brother walked in carrying the fish and chips with a stupid grin on his face, it turned out that he had been the one in the bushes and both him and my mother seemed to think it was funny and that I was a big baby.

III

Another four weeks and we would have a new baby. I was really getting excited about how lovely it would be.

It had been decided that my brother would go to my grandparents who had now left the pub as my grandmother's drinking had started to become a problem. I was going to my auntie's two doors away from where we lived. Well, she was not really my auntie, but we had always called her that. She had two boys, the youngest my brother's age, and I liked him because he would always stick up for me when my brother wouldn't let me play with them. It was pretty good now as Mam had finished work and she was there before we went to school with the fire lit and breakfast ready. It meant we didn't have to get up so early.

The other good thing was we could have her bike to ride quite often. My brother had it the most of course, being the elder, but I loved it when I could have it and used to take myself off on bike rides. I would go up to a friend's farm and we had loads of fun playing in the barns and all the fields, a different life to what I had known and her mam and dad were lovely. The other good thing was that Mother would let me stay at school for dinner now she was home all the time, which meant I didn't get into trouble with the teachers so much. Life was pretty good.

One day at lunchtime a gang of us went down to the old mill, which was fun, though dangerous really, as it was disused. When I returned I discovered Mother had gone to hospital and I was to stay at my auntie's, as my father had always taken the view that the children were the responsibility of the mother. I always loved going to my auntie's, we got to have sauce on our fried bread for breakfast, which was considered a luxury at home. My cousin and I would use the arms of the chairs to sit on when we were playing cowboys and Indians and she wouldn't tell us off, in fact she seemed to think we were funny! *Why couldn't my mother be like this?*

She would take us to bed at night and tuck us in with a kiss goodnight – *Is this how it's supposed to be?*

She would also let me read and, even better, I would be allowed to keep the light on all night, I was not as frightened there.

We finally heard that I had a little baby brother and mother was due to come home in ten days. I'd have much rather stopped with my auntie, but I was looking forward to seeing my new brother. There weren't many cars then and few people had one. I was lucky really because granddad came down and took me to the hospital to see my mam and new brother. He was so tiny and cute! I couldn't wait to get him home.

Time passed by and I had some lovely days and even better nights staying at my auntie's. We were allowed to stay up late at the weekend as there was no school there.

Mother and my baby brother would be coming home the next day and Granddad was going to collect them, so it was my last night there. It was funny how I never seemed to get into trouble there, perhaps my auntie was more tolerant then my mother.

Well, it was back to normal at home except that there was no shouting or bad tempers, I wondered how long it would last. The baby was lovely, I was going to love him to bits. Mother let me hold him and he was really good. My big brother seemed quite indifferent to him, but then he was not really bothered about babies. He slept in a drawer on two chairs next to my parents' bed, they hadn't purchased a cot yet.

Mother seemed a lot happier now she had the baby and Father was being very good. He still hadn't given his nights out up, but at least he was not being violent. Mother soon showed me how to change nappies. They were all towelling ones then; the only thing I was not keen on was having to wash them out after he'd done a job, but it was all a part of it I suppose. It's funny how she taught me that, but would never let me help her to bake or anything like that. She always said she couldn't take the time and wanted to get the job done and I was more of a hindrance then a help.

One day Mother let me take the baby out for a little walk in his pram. Unfortunately, I had just got round the corner and the pram wheels went off one side of the kerb and the pram tipped over sideways. I picked it up and the baby seemed OK and my mother came running round the corner; someone had already told her that the pram had been tipped up. Why did I do try and bluff my way out of it? I was in for a good hiding, but she seemed to believe me so I got off with that one. It put me off a bit because the pram was too large for me to handle. Still I got to cuddle him in the evening when he liked been rocked to sleep.

Only another six months to go then I went up to the big school. It was a bit frightening as it was rather large, but I daren't say I was scared about it as I'd only be called a big baby.

Then one Saturday night, they started. They hadn't been too bad, but it sounded like a big one. Mother ran down stairs and I could hear Father following her for the screams that she was getting beaten. *God, why do I have to listen to this?* I remember thinking. *I wish he would go out and never come back again.* Now the baby was crying, poor little lad. He didn't know what he'd come into. Mother went back up to see to him, and Father followed. All went quiet.

That Sunday, Mother said she would take us fishing and swimming down the beck and told us we could have a picnic as Father would be away with his friends for the day. I couldn't swim, but mother and my big brother said they would teach me, which was good, or so I thought at the time.

It was a lovely warm day for the time of year and there were quite a few kids at the beck. Most of them were swimming. One girl called Constance swam with my brother; I liked her, she seemed fun, but Mother said she was bad and I had better not associate with her – typical! I just paddled about for a while, then they said they would teach me to swim before we had our sandwiches. Mother went in the beck with my brother and held out her hands. I had no sooner reached out when she pulled me in and pushed me under the water, it was deep, dark and I could see the fishes swimming about, I couldn't breathe. *Please god let her get me up.*

All the kids plus Mother and my brother laughed at me and said that was the best way to learn and I was a great big baby. Perhaps I am, because all I know is that I was very frightened and I have never wanted to go near the water again. I ran off crying when I got out on the bank. I came back eventually to get dressed when I thought they had all stopped laughing at me. Well, everyone had except Mother who seemed to think that she could still teach me to swim. Not stopping to find out I ran off and met Constance on the way home. I arranged to meet her later if I could get out, I didn't care what anyone said – she was good fun and would cheer me up anyway. I sat on the swing in the garden till they came home because I couldn't go down to the beck again in case they got me.

Mother came home about four, perhaps I'd get something to eat now. I was pretty hungry. It was my own fault, I really should have joined the picnic, but hadn't dared. Boy, was she in a bad mood with me for running off. I can't blame her really. She bathed the baby and put him to bed. My big brother went out to play. *Maybe I could have some food now*, I thought, *I haven't eaten since breakfast*. Wishful thinking! She got the sweeping brush and did she lay into me. Every strike was followed by shouts of 'I'll teach you to run away from me!'

She sent me out to get some coal in and I realised I could escape a further beating. I left the bucket and ran from the house. By chance I ran into Constance, and we decided to go down for a walk in the fields. At least she made me laugh. Her life sounded totally different from mine.

I didn't even think about what I was going to do after we'd finished messing about, but the decision was taken out off my hands by the appearance of my brother. He chased us, shouting that Mother had sent him to fetch me home and would I be in for it when I got back.

We managed to give him the slip and Constance said she knew where I could go for the night and she would fetch me something to eat later on. We walked up to a field where there was a barn full of hay. Constance said to stop there and she would be back soon. It was very dark inside and I was scared of that, but more scared to go home. Constance was soon back with some food, thank heavens, I was very hungry. She said she would return after school the following day with some more food.

The night seemed to last for ever. At one point I heard voices and it sounded like my mother so I buried myself under the hay. I must have fallen asleep at some time because when I woke up it was daylight. I didn't have a clue what time it was, so I decided to go for a little walk round, not knowing that the police had been all around the area with my photograph and there were some hawkers in the lay-by at the bottom of the field where I had been staying.

I ran right into them and one of them grabbed me by the arm. I tried to tell them it wasn't me that they were looking for but my twin sister, but they certainly didn't believe that. They put me in the van and took me to the police station where I was asked why I had run away. What could I tell them? If I told them that I had been beaten and frightened, Mother would beat me twice as bad when she got me home. I just said I didn't know why I had done it.

I got a big lecture off the police that I could have been murdered and my parents were out of there minds with worry about me plus look at all the trouble I had caused them. I couldn't win. They took me home to Mother who did seem concerned about me so I did feel awful about all the trouble I had caused. She gave me a lovely breakfast and bath and packed me off to bed. I felt so loved and wanted at that time that I quickly forgot why I had run away in the first place.

Monday morning it was back to school as if the weekend hadn't happened at all. I was pleased to be going back to school though, I used to enjoy my lessons and it was much better now I didn't have to come home. Sometimes mother would even let me take her bike to school, which was better still as it cut out the amount of walking I had to do.

Even though I only went to the hospital now for check-ups I still suffered at night with aching legs. Sometimes I would cry myself to sleep because I couldn't stand it. All the doctors said was it was growing pains and that it would pass.

Night-times after school I would be allowed to go out for about an hour to play. Most of the time I would go round the back through the fields and would talk to imaginary people and just live in a make-believe word where everything was perfect and I was loved by the various people that were in my make-believe world. I got in trouble often for coming in late, but I didn't mind so much because I would only get grounded and not hit. Soon it would be time for the summer holidays and light nights and then I would be able to go to my friend's farm and play and go out on the bike for rides, away from home.

I came in from school one night and everyone seemed very quiet. It felt like something wasn't quite right, Father hadn't a lot to say and he hadn't gone out for a couple of nights, which was odd because usually he went out every night.

We soon found out that Father had lost his job and there was a big shortage of money. Mother was very worried about having the baby to feed. Of course Father would get dole money, but that wasn't a lot compared to what he could earn. You'd have thought he would give his pub trips up, but no. All their rows now revolved around money and he beat her regularly. We were lucky, I suppose, because mother had always made loads of jam and for a while we lived on jam and bread. On the third day after he lost his job my father turned up with flowers for my mother and sweets for us and say how sorry he was. He was full of remorse and swore it would never happen again. How many times had that had been said, I don't know. He said it was the frustration of not been able to work; it could have being I suppose, as I had never known my dad to be out of work.

My granddad, since leaving the pub, had built up a small building firm and he had quite a bit of work on, and said that my father could come and work for him if it would improve things. So that is how my father ended up working for my grandfather.

IV

Mother returned home that evening and things soon slipped back into normal or as normal as my life could be.

I hadn't been home long when mother told us she was pregnant again. The other little one was only three months old, so there was not the same excitement with this one. I only thought of all the extra nappies and how could I rock two babies to sleep. I never talked to Mam about any of this, in fact, I never talked to her about anything, she was not a person you could talk to.

I got myself a newspaper round. In those days it didn't matter how old you were, and I thought it would help mother with money and pay her back for raising me. If she was grateful, I'll never know; all I knew was I would do anything for a bit of praise, anything to please her. The paper round brought in seven shillings and sixpence, which I thought was wonderful and I was doing something to pay Mam back.

Like when I used to go sticking for hedge sticks, the more I got in the coalhouse the happier I felt. I used to make a sling out of string and carry them on my back. I don't think I ever received any thanks, but I was certain that there must be something I could do that would please her.

Mother must have been finding it hard work as she kept me off school to help her. I mainly had to run about getting her polish and things when she was upstairs.

One time I brought the wrong thing up for her and got a smack round the head, but I slipped and there was lino on the top of the stairs and I went sliding into the door frame. The left side of my forehead came right up and Mother was so worried she put me to bed and said she was going to get the doctor. I can't remember much, except that to this day if I get a bump on that part of my head it hurts. I think I spent about a week in bed. I can remember one thing and that's when Mam was talking to my auntie out of my bedroom window while cleaning it and she told her how I'd wet the bed last night. I felt like a big baby and wished she hadn't told her or she would never want me to stop there again.

I went back to school the following week. Most of the gang that I went to the mill with on a lunchtime had started smoking, so they soon had me joining in. I was very soon addicted to cigs, but the problem was I didn't have any money to feed my new habit. I would run errands for the neighbours to get money and when that didn't work I stole my mother's cigs. Sometimes when I had to go shopping for her, I would add a little extra on each time for cigs. I am not proud of it even though five Woodbines only cost about two pence. I still did my paper round each morning, but I could never ask Mam for any of that as she now considered it to be hers.

I also had my first boyfriend, not that I knew anything about boys. It just made me feel like the rest of them. He was a nice boy called Jimmy. There was another boy called Alan who also wanted to go around with me, which made me feel good and wanted. All innocent just arms round each other and a quick kiss now and then.

I would soon be at the big school now and Mother was getting my uniform together. I felt really good in the blazer, but the only problem was that I had to wear a skirt and I didn't like skirts. However, trousers weren't allowed.

I found a good place to hide my cigs by unscrewing the dynamo of the front of Mam's bike and putting them and the matches in there, then screwing it back up again. No one could tell there was anything in there. This soon backfired on me when one day my brother took the bike and the dynamo, and all my little horde fell off. He couldn't wait to tell Mam. Of course, I denied it. She said that if ever she caught me smoking she would ram every cigarette down my throat lit or not. I would have to be more careful.

I was allowed to go and stay with my gran on my last holidays before I went to the big school. She was strict insomuch as that she expected me to do a lot of chores, but I usually had the afternoon to myself. It was just a little village with maybe twelve houses at the most, but I used to spend my time in the fields and by the water. These holidays were quite good because one of the neighbours had her niece staying so we played together. She liked the fields too, which was just as well because there wasn't much else to do there.

One day we went to the field with the horses where the niece goaded me to sit on the back of one. I thought she wouldn't like me if I didn't, so I climbed on the fence and jumped on the horse's back. Well, it set off round the field hell for leather, me hanging on for grim death. Scared stiff I was; it eventually threw me over its back. I picked myself up and did my arm hurt when I tried to put it behind my back! But I thought nothing of it and went home for tea. Gran asked what was the matter, but I said nothing, I didn't know what she would be like with me.

Thank God she never checked me at bedtime, because I couldn't move my arm to get undressed properly and just hoped it would be better tomorrow. When I got up the next morning I couldn't get my arm from behind my back. Of course, Gran then questioned me and I had to tell her what had happened.

Granddad drove down to get my mam, and Gran looked after the bairn while they took me to hospital. It turned out that I had fractured it so I ended up in plaster, of course I now had to go home.

Well, after all that I started the big school. It was massive and we had to walk to different classrooms for our lessons, I enjoyed it once I got settled in.

Mother was due to have the other baby soon and was very tired towards the end so I had an awful lot to do, both at lunchtime and of an evening. The first baby was now nearly nine months old and he was very good, small and cute, I loved cuddling him of an evening.

I made some new friends at the school, but didn't quite understand their conversations sometimes about boys and things, but seemed to bluff my way through things. Constance was there and she had a friend called Pat – they were a good laugh, never serious about anything. We used to hate the sewing lesson so we sat at the back of the class and fooled about – we were always in trouble in that lesson. We used to have a gardening lesson and we could go round the back of the shed and have a smoke, as both

Constance and Pat smoked too. Two girls at the school were a shilling short of a pound and we had great pleasure in tormenting them. If I could make them cry on the way home I would be highly delighted – what an evil little child I was really.

There was another girl there who was very popular. They called her May She was very pretty and I for one would have given anything to look like her. She had quite a following, in fact it was called May's Gang. No one ever crossed her. I can remember one occasion on my way home the gang had a go at me, I can't remember what it was about, but I do know that they kept pushing me over and laughing because I was crying, and calling me a big baby.

It was only one occasion and after that May seemed to be OK with me; perhaps she knew I worshipped her from afar. So I stuck with the bad lot as Mother called them. She told me to keep away from them, but the more you're told not to, the more you do.

Mother planned to have the next baby at home so I was now kept off school to look after the house and my young brother. The next one was a boy also, I wished I could have a little sister, it would have been interesting to find out if Mother only liked boys, because I came to the conclusion that she hated me. I told her I thought that she must have adopted me because she didn't love me. That got me another good hiding.

The baby was lovely. He was a little chubby chap and later on the two babies looked like twins, one small and one chubby. I loved them both dearly, in fact most of my love went on them, they couldn't hurt me or so I thought at that time. I went around with a boy called Alan then, suppose you could say he was my boyfriend. All I know was that he used to put his arm round me and make me feel special, and if anyone picked on me, he would always be there to defend me.

When I went to bed at night I used to talk to May and another girl that I thought was nice. The worrying thing I suppose is that they used to talk back to me, but they would say what I wanted them to say because it was me doing all the talking of course.

I didn't know why I felt like this at the time and it took me many years and soul searching before I even knew or would accept what it was all about. I still did my paper round and tipped the money up to Mother; I was sure there must be something else I could do to pay her back. The reason I felt this way was because she told me I owed her for my upbringing.

I started collecting rags after school, I could make ten shillings every fortnight, used to have to wheel them on the boogie one and a half miles to get the money, but surely mother would be pleased. Instead: no response; she just accepted the money without saying a word.

I went and did work on the local farm occasionally and picked potatoes during the picking time. It was funny how my big brother managed to keep all his money; still, another year and he would be starting work. It had been decided that he would go and work for my granddad when he left school, as my father no longer worked for him but had a job with a local building firm.

I cannot remember why I got this particular beating, but I do remember she hit me with the poker and my arm came up with a huge mark across it. She sent me up to the local hospital and told me to tell them that the shed door had slammed shut on my hand, one day perhaps I wouldn't be scared to tell them the truth, who knows.

I was now thirteen years old, my big brother was at work, and the young ones were three and just over two years old. I took them out to the park one day where there was a small paddling pool. Bert, the youngest, went into it with all his clothes on while I wasn't watching, I had to walked them round the fields until he was dry or so I thought.

It didn't work like that. When we got home Mother got him ready for his bath and his vest happened to be wet underneath his clothes. She beat me with the hair brush on that occasion, in fact she kept on until the brush broke and I didn't think I could cry any more; *why does she hate me so much?*

My elder brother seemed to be causing a few problems now he had started work, so Mother asked my father to have a word with him, but he really didn't want to know. All he said he wanted was a bit of peace and quiet in the home.

My brother came home blind drunk one night and my mother and I had to undress him and put him to bed. He never got into trouble for it, in fact Mother seemed to think that it was funny.

The times she was annoyed with him didn't seem to matter much to him, in fact he'd just kick the pegs all over the porch in a temper. He must have been watching Father too much I guess.

Father at this time worked for a chap who was responsible for the building of a big new supermarket in the town. His boss was a man called Sid and he lived in a caravan at the back of the site for the supermarket. He was a family man and went home most weekends to Nottingham where he lived with his wife and daughter. Mam soon got involved by doing his washing, after all it was money for her, Fred was not the kind of chap to take something for nothing.

He was a really nice person and I got on well with him when he occasionally came to our house for a meal. Perhaps it was due to the fact that his daughter was only a year older than me. Father soon saw a chance there and before I knew what was what I found myself been roped in to clean Fred's caravan twice a week. I was very nervous at first because I would be by myself and I guessed he would think I was a bit of an idiot, I didn't think much of myself really. I shouldn't have worried, he was lovely. He would pay me and then give me something extra for myself, it was like he knew that what he paid me went straight to Mother. He would say that was our secret and then laugh, I was not used to anyone being that nice.

One week he asked my parents if I could go home with him as I would be company for him on the drive down and company for his daughter at the weekend. I didn't think for a minute that they would let me go but surprisingly they did. I was worried about meeting his wife and daughter, but didn't have to be as they were just as nice as him! I shared a bedroom with Yvette and couldn't believe that we were allowed to smoke in there. The only thing I felt embarrassed about was getting undressed. I was rather shy about things like that, still am, what with all the scars on my leg.

That goes back to when I was about ten years old and we were at the beach and I heard a comment passed by some women saying, 'Look at that poor little girl's leg.'

I need not have worried because we just got ready for bed owing to the fact that it was my first night there. Yvette said we would go out tomorrow night, just us, and her dad said he was taking me shopping the next day for something to go out in. I could understand why when I saw Yvette's wardrobe. The next day started with Yvette's mother fetching us tea in bed and we lay there and had a cig before we got up. This was the life for real.

We then went out shopping. You should have seen the outfit and the shoes he bought me, I thought I would never walk in them, but all the family made me feel at ease.

Yvette and I went out that evening, we went to a dance club, I couldn't believe how different things were compared to where I lived. I felt like a fish out of water, but everyone was really nice and she had loads of friends. Bet they had a good laugh about the country bumpkin afterwards. We didn't get in until the early hours of the morning. I was tired out as my bedtime was nine each evening at home. Yvette said that we didn't have to get up next morning, it seemed like she didn't have chores or anything to do except have a good time and live her life, her parents loved her to bits, I couldn't tell her much about my life as she would think I was a fool, back to the real world tomorrow.

The journey back home was fine, no more cigs now as it was back home, I would have to be sneaky again. I was still on cloud nine when I got home, but that soon altered. I showed Mother my new clothes and shoes. You should have heard the comment on those, I didn't feel special for very long.

V

Back to the paper round, rag collecting and cleaning Fred's caravan. Fred told me he would be leaving soon as he was wanted elsewhere, I would miss him as he was one of the only people that treated me as if I was a person with thoughts of my own.

Life went on pretty much the same really – drunken nights with Father, beatings from Mother, and plenty of clips round the earhole for me. Mother kept me off school again to help her, but this time she was quite patient with me. She was weird sometimes; she would say that she had a funny feeling that something was going to happen. I didn't pay much attention to her, but one lunchtime my brother came home after a visit to the hospital, he had had an accident at work and had taken off the tip of his finger. I said to Mother that she was right about something happening, but she said, 'No that's not it.'

I had just got all the housework done when there was a knock on the door, a telegram had arrived from my uncle down south, the one we always went to at Christmas. It said that my auntie had been killed in an accident. I didn't believe it. *She just wants to see us so this is her way of getting us there*; funny what you think when you don't want to believe something.

My two young brothers were to go to my grandparents and my elder brother wanted to stay at home. How could he? My parents were taking me with them, fine, I would soon see my auntie again. We travelled down by train during the night and reached there early morning, all the way down I kept telling myself that it was a joke and she only wanted to see me. I realised when I got there and there was only my uncle that it was true. How could God take her away from me? She had been getting off a bus and trying to cross the road home when a car with a boat on a trailer had caught her on one of the hooks and swung her backwards and forwards against a wall. They say every bone in her body was broken.

The funeral was to be in two days and she was coming home the night before to be laid out in the best room for viewing. I was given supper and packed off to bed, everyone else went out to the pub. I'll never understand that even to this day it seems like a death is an excuse to drink.

The next day seemed like any other day except that there were a lot of visitors coming and going. That evening they brought my auntie home in a coffin and placed her on chairs in the best room, Mother asked me if I wanted to see her, what a stupid question. I was slightly nervous, but once I went in the room with her all I wanted to do was hug her and tell her how much I loved her, that they couldn't take her away from me.

My uncle showed me a drawer and in this drawer there was every present I had ever bought her all carefully wrapped up in tissue paper. She did love me as much as I loved her.

Mother said I couldn't go to her funeral the next day even though I begged and pleaded with her. She said I had to look after the little boy next door while they went to the funeral, and told me not to be so bloody selfish. What does she know; it was times like this when I really wished I could hate her. Perhaps that's been the problem all along: whatever she did to me, I worshipped the ground she walked on and spent my life trying to get her to love me, or even give me a cuddle, in fact any little crumb would have done.

So I took the little boy down to the wreck, as it was called, little knowing that the cortege came by that way to the cemetery. The child was about two and a half years old and not a bad kid. I saw them go by with my auntie and what I did next will stay with me for the rest of my life. I was crying my eyes out and the child was asking to go on the swings. We were standing at the edge of a steep grassy bank and, what did I do, I pushed him down the hill. He must have thought it was a game at first, I suppose, but as soon as his little legs had brought him to the top I pushed him back down again. I must have done this a few times, I don't really know, all I knew was that I wanted my auntie back and she'd gone. Something clicked when he came back up the hill sobbing his little heart out, *God what have I done to the poor little lad?* I loved him and cried with him he soon recovered, but I felt like a complete monster – was I like my mother? Please don't let me be like that.

They all came back to the house for tea; funny, isn't it, how after a funeral everyone seems to be happy and hungry, all that talk, as if she never existed? Then all the men went off to the pub and drink themselves senseless, mind they're pretty senseless when they are sober. So that was all over, I hoped I could feel like she would always be there. As far as I was concerned as long as I lived I would always remember her.

Back home the next morning, as Father had to get back to work and we couldn't leave the young ones with my grandparents for too long. Well, at least I could love them when we were home, they loved being cuddled, especially Bert, the youngest. He was so cute, he still had a chubby face and there was something about him, a Little-Boy-Lost look. He never looked like the rest of us, we all have brown eyes and the same features, but he was always different.

I remember Father beating Mother that year, and saying that Bert wasn't his child – fat chance of that, she never goes anywhere except with the children. One Sunday, Father came home from the pub and asked my mother to put the kids in the pram and they would go for a walk – something was wrong, that was unheard of. So off we all went for a family walk. I was right. He only wanted the pram and the false bottom to put copper wire in that he had hidden when he'd been working, a bit more money for his beer, how I hated him and wished he would die.

Life soon got back to normal, well as normal as it could be in our household. Something happened to me and even though I was fourteen years old, I didn't know what was going on. I thought I had injured myself on the bike, it turned out that I had just started my period. All Mother did was give me STs and say to me that this would happen every month and keep away from boys. I didn't have a clue what she was on about. I remember the girls going round school asking if you were a virgin, but as I didn't know what they meant I just laughed and passed it off and that seemed to work.

It was shortly after we returned home from the south that my mother said that she was pregnant again, I wondered if I would get a sister this time. I seemed to be surrounded by males. It would be about six months into her pregnancy when it started to happen. Mother had taken the kids to the park for the afternoon and she said that I had to stay in and make my father's cup of tea and get his dinner out of the oven when he came in from the pub. That much was fine, after all he had to be waited on hand and foot.

He came in, usual time after the pub had closed of course and asked were Mother was, and I told him she had gone to the park with the bairns. He asked me how long she had been gone and I told him she had left about an hour ago. He seemed fine with that, in fact he was in quite a good mood, laughing and fooling about. I didn't know he could be funny like that, but now I could see why everyone thought he was a nice guy. He sat downstairs with the newspapers, which was unusual as he normally went to bed after he'd had his dinner.

I guess I'd started washing up when Father said, wasn't I a good girl and a real help to my mother. There was never praise in this house – something was wrong. He then came up behind me and put his arms round me, he then put his hands on my breasts, I asked him not to do that, please, he replied that it was OK and no one would ever know, it would be just our little secret. I told him I didn't like it, with that his hand went between my legs and he said that if I said anything, he would tell my mother that I hadn't looked after him properly at dinner time and then I'd know what would happen. What could I do? I had no one to talk to and Mother would beat me if she thought I'd been awkward with my father. This is what they call love in this house, is it? *Please go to bed and leave me alone.* He eventually went off and left me. I had to get out of there, so went down to my favourite place by the water. I sat there wondering what I could do, I didn't really know what I felt, perhaps I could just forget about it. I couldn't tell anyone because, even if I had anyone to tell, they wouldn't believe me. After all, I was just a problem child, so Mother always told me after I had run away.

I was very late home that night, I didn't really want to go home, but had nowhere else to go.

Mother went spare when I got home, I told her that I had

fallen to sleep and didn't know what time it was. Of course it doesn't need a genius to see that I got a good hiding. Father had gone back out to the pub again by this time.

Shortly after that incident mother was taken ill with flu and she coughed and cracked a rib so she had to stay in bed, I must admit that she must have been ill because she was not one to stay in bed. I was kept off school to run the house under her guidance and look after the two boys. It was hard work getting meals, washing and running up and down stairs making sure Mother was OK. My father and big brother still expected their meals on the table when they came in and my brother certainly didn't do anything to help.

It was a Friday night and I had got the boys settled into bed. Father had gone to the pub as usual and I took Mother a drink and asked her if I could go to bed as I was very tired. My bedroom was next door to mam's so I told her if she wanted anything just to shout and I would hear her.

When I woke up, I don't know what time it was, but my father had his hands under the bedcovers touching me. I asked him please not to do that, but I was scared my mother would hear and come in and beat me. What could I do? It hurt and I was sure it should not be happening to me. I couldn't get back to sleep as I was scared he would come back in again. I heard him arguing with Mother then it all seemed to go quiet.

The next day I was very tired and Mother said I had to get my act together as the doctor would be coming to see her later on. So much to do, I got the washing done, but it was raining so I put it on the clothes horse round the fire and cleaned up everything before the doctor arrived. When he came downstairs after seeing Mother he said that she could get up for a while, but to take it easy and how lucky she was to have me. I wished she thought so.

I built the fire up and made a cup of tea and told the boys to play with their toys and not to bother Mother when she came down, then I told her she could come down for a while as everything was done.

She came downstairs and I thought she would be pleased with me. I knew I couldn't do things as well as her, but I thought I had done all right and the doctor seemed to think I was good, so why wouldn't she? She came through to the room and on her way through ran her hand over the furniture, said 'Look at the dust here' and flashed her hand at me. She then went round the house finding fault with everything, pushed the clothes horse over and stamped on all the clothes.

The room had a partition separating the kitchen and there was a small corner which she pushed me into. She then picked up the poker from the hearth and laid into me with it. When I couldn't cry any more she said, 'I am going back upstairs and will be down in half an hour; if this is not all cleaned up properly by then you will get the same again.'

To think I was so happy because she was allowed to get up. Well, what could I do? I knew that it was impossible to clean everything to her satisfaction in the allotted time and I knew that I didn't want a beating like that again so I told the little ones to play till Mother came down and be good, and that I would miss them.

I put my duffel coat on and ran for my life. I didn't know where I was going at that time, I just knew I had to get away. It was freezing cold, the middle of February and here I was out on a limb. I needed to think.

I decided that I would try and make my way through to Fred's, I guessed he would want to help me. I had a rough idea of the way there so I set off. I was very tired and hungry, but had no money and daren't stop for fear my brother would come after me. I'd got about ten miles when a wagon stopped and, what did I do, but run over the nearest hedge and lay down in the snow at the bottom of the hedge, hoping he wouldn't look for me, but drive on.

I don't know how long I lay there, but I felt wet and cold and it must have been quite late. I just hoped no one else would stop and I could carry on. I started walking again and heard a noise coming from behind me, I couldn't see anything. Boy, was I scared, it seemed to be the worst of two evils: dark vs. Mother.

It turned out that there was a man walking behind me pushing a bike. He soon caught up to me and chatted away. He asked where I was going and I told him I was going to my auntie's as my parents had gone away. I said that I had lost my purse hence the fact that I was walking. When he found all this out he said I could go home with him for the evening and get off again early next morning. I said, 'No thank you, my auntie would be worried.' On my reply he got nasty and tried to grab hold of me, so I shot over the nearest hedge and ran. I could hear him following me and shouting abuse. *Are all men like this?* I asked myself. He must have given up so I lay there for what seemed like ages and when I could hear nothing came out on the road again.

I had been walking for what seemed like ages, and I was wet, cold and very hungry. Another wagon pulled up. *What the heck*, I thought, *I don't even care now; they could do what they wanted. Everyone else seems to.* So I told the man the same tale as the man with the bike, but told him I needed to get to Nottingham. He said I was way off track, but that he would take me as far as Sheffield and show me where to get another lift to Nottingham. He seemed OK, but then so did the other guy. We stopped at a café for transport drivers and he told me to wait in the cab and that he would fetch me something to eat. I must have dozed off because next thing he was back with food for me, did I enjoy that.

He asked me how old I was, all these questions. I told him I was sixteen and he said that I didn't look that old, said he had a daughter who was fifteen years old and a twelve-year-old son. He really seemed nice, but I wouldn't be fooled.

I fell asleep and slept most of the way. We arrived in Sheffield in the early hours of the morning and he told me that if I walked down these streets I would meet up with the early morning drivers and they would take me the rest of the way. Little did I know that once he had dropped me off he went to the police station and informed them that he thought he had given a runaway a lift. I was picked up wandering round Sheffield and taken to the police station.

Of course I tried to fool them with the same tale I had spun the driver, but they weren't as easily fooled and told me they knew I had run away so I might as well make it easy on myself and tell them where I came from and what my name was. No choice really, so I told them. They asked me why I had left and I couldn't tell them, so I was in trouble with them again.

They took me to this house where all the bad girls were; well, that made me feel really good, I can tell you. The girls were not very friendly and neither was the woman in charge, she told me my mother was coming by train to pick me up and gave me a lecture about all the trouble I had caused, little did she know. *There must be some way out.* Mother arrived all sweetness and charm, laying it on to the police about how I'd done it before and that I was a problem. Of course she got all the sympathy because she was pregnant. The women in the house said that I probably needed a damned good hiding; no doubt I would get one when we got home.

The police took us to the railway station. Mother started as soon as the train began to move about how much money I had cost her and how she would make sure I paid for it. *God I wish I was dead.* After she had ranted for a while all went quiet and she never spoke to me for the rest of the journey.

When we arrived home she said that she had to take me up to the police station. Did I get it in the neck from the police about wasting their time and how if I wasn't careful I would end up being taken away. I wish they had taken me away, no one wanted me at home.

Well, another few months and I would leave school, the next thing that came up on the horizon was the school taking me to juvenile court because of all my time off. Great. It wasn't even my fault. I got three months probation for that little incident, and lectures right, left and centre.

Mother by this time was eight months pregnant and things were very hard at home. I had lots more work to do and things didn't change as regards my father touching me whenever he got the chance. I worked out that if I left my wardrobe door open slightly at night it would wedge against my bedroom door and he couldn't get in while I was asleep. So he told mother I was too cheeky to him and that I needed straightening up, well, believe me, she didn't need a reason to beat me, but Father said that now I knew he could soon get me into trouble and that I had better be nice to him. So it got worse, if that could be possible. Every chance my father got he would be at me and each time he would go a bit further and would expose himself to me with comments about what I could do for him.

One night he came in and Mother wouldn't give him what he

wanted, so even though she was eight months pregnant he got her in the corner and gave her a good beating. I soon went downstairs to see if she was OK, I felt really sorry for her, why did she stay? I asked her why she didn't leave him and she said that it was because of the children. She was ill the next day and had to go to the doctors for a check-up. The doctor was not very happy because she had bruising on her stomach and she had to tell him the truth that my father had beaten her the night before.

About a fortnight later she went into labour and a policeman came down and told my father that if my mother lost her life or she lost the child that they would have him on a charge of manslaughter. He was frantic after they left, ranting and raving like a madman. Both the bairns were upset and crying, so he had a go at them. I took them into the bedroom out of his way and eventually got them calmed down and off to sleep. Then I carried them off to bed poor little mites.

The midwife soon came down and told my father he had a daughter and I had a new little sister and my mother was all right and we could go up and see them soon, after ever thing was cleared away. Talk about relieved. That night he'd got away with it.

We went up to see my sister and of course my father was very sorry, he always was after he'd beaten her, he said that as soon as she was up and about he would take her out and treat her. God he must have been worried.

My little sister was lovely, but the funny thing was that she had bruising on her face and it looked exactly like the marks as my auntie had when she was killed in the accident. Because of this they decided to call her after my auntie. I wondered if that would be the end of babies, not that I minded because I loved them all very much. In fact, sometimes they were the only thing that kept me going through it all.

Things soon returned back to normal, or as normal as they could be in that house.

VI

Another two weeks and I would leave school as I was fifteen years old now. Mother told me that she had got me a job at the grocery store in the town and I would start the day after I left school. She also informed me that my wages had to come home to her and I wasn't to open my pay packet. Why was that when my brother was allowed to keep his? When he started work he gave my mother what he thought she should have and the rest he kept.

It was Sunday and Mother had gone out with the kids, with the usual story that I had to stay in and look after my pig of a father. I knew what was coming or at least I thought I did. Biggest mistake in my life. I should have known by now that there was always something worse round the corner. He came in as usual, for his dinner and all chatty as usual, I had to get out of the way as quickly as possible. He started and the treats came fast and furious, but this time he went further and forced himself on me I was crying and asking him to stop as he was hurting me he said that if I relaxed and laid still like a good girl it wouldn't hurt and that he would give me some money to treat myself. I didn't want anything, just for him to stop hurting me. He eventually got off and marched off to bed telling me that if I said anything I would be in big trouble as no one would believe a little liar like me.

I went out down the fields; perhaps it would be better when I started work. I got down the fields to find out that I was bleeding and sore, I knew it wasn't my period time so could only think it was because of my father. How would I get round this? My mother kept strict tabs on when my period was. I would have to get home late and tell her that I had slipped in some cow dirt – that way I could rinse my trousers out and put them on the line when I got in. Luckily when I got in, Mother had already gone to bed, the door was unlocked for my elder brother so I managed to wash my things out.

I crept off to bed, remembering to wedge my bedroom door,

and hoped he would leave me alone that night. I cried myself to sleep, silently, so that no one would hear me. My little brothers slept in my elder brother's room and I knew he wasn't in so I crept out of bed just to give them a love and let them know I wouldn't let anyone hurt them. They were fast asleep of course, but that didn't matter. Luckily Mother believed the tale and that explanation as to why my trousers were on the line. She never even questioned when I came in.

It would soon be time for me to leave school and then, I thought, things might alter. I was a bit nervous about starting work. Mother took me up to the shop before I started there and the manager seemed OK. There was another girl starting the same time as me. Well, I finally left school and promised to keep in touch with Constance and Pat, after all they only lived around the corner.

I walked up to the shop the next day and waited outside the back door for it to open, it wouldn't do to be late on the first day. All the staff arrived and the under manager – he looked like a bit of a hard taskmaster, but once I got to know him he wasn't all that bad. He only asked that things were done properly and that was fair enough. There was an old woman – well, she seemed old to me – and she looked a bit sour faced, she never smiled and quite often snapped at us, though I found out later that she wasn't too bad, that was just her way.

The other girl and I were both juniors. In the shop we had all the boring jobs to do and certainly were not allowed to have anything to do with the customers. In those days everything in the shop was put up on the scales – sugar, fruit, lard, even the biscuits were all loose in a big display. We were allowed to make up the boxes for delivery to the customers, I really enjoyed it.

The job that I enjoyed most was working in the cellar with a lady called Joan. We used to have separate scales and weighed up blocks of lard into pounds and wrapped them in greaseproof paper. She said that I was very good at it and there weren't many people that could get it spot on without a lot of cutting up. She would always request me down there to work with her. I guess I had a crush on her because I thought she was wonderful.

Things seemed a little bit better at home now that I was

working; I still had things to do, but didn't mind that too much because it was usually with my little sister and brothers. They were growing up now, but I still felt close to them. The boys looked just like twins and mother dressed them pretty much alike. They were so funny and I had many a laugh with them. One night Mother said the baby was crying so I ran upstairs, but when I got there she was fast asleep. I got out of the bedroom and at the top of the stairs the lights went off and I was too scared to move any further. Then the bedroom door at the bottom of the stairs started to creak, so I just sat on the top of the stairs and cried for my mother to get the lights on again. She just shouted back not to be stupid and get myself down before I woke the kids up. I couldn't move, I was too scared. Then the lights came back on and my elder brother came out of the room, laughing his head off. My mother was laughing also, they seemed to find it amusing that I was scared to death.

Things didn't alter much with Father and every time Mother wasn't available for his needs, I got it. He came in one Sunday and asked Mother to go down to the fields with him and collect a big saw that he had hidden after stealing it. Mother said that she was too tired to go out and that he should take me with him and I would help him. Of course I didn't have any choice in the matter, so we set off on the bikes. It took about ten minutes to get to the fields; we then had to walk across two fields to get to the place were he had hidden the saw. The field over from where we were had two caravans in it and I believed someone lived in them. We had to go under some barbwire to get the saw out of the hedge, Father kept the chat up across the fields, saying how nice it was that I was helping him instead of my mother, he must have known that I didn't have a choice. And I guess I knew what was about to happen to me.

On the way back as we were just about to get under the barbed wire he started. I must have felt brave that day, but later on I wish I'd just taken it. I don't know which was the worst, Mother's beatings or Father's rape.

As I crept under the wire he made a grab for me and I told him if he touched me I would scream and the caravan people would hear me. I guess he didn't believe me because he still kept grabbing at me. I screamed and then got stuck on the barbed wire, Father kicked me and cursed me saying, 'Wait until you get home, will you suffer for this, girl.' And suffer I did. Father cursed me all the way home, telling me how he'd get even.

When we got home he told my mother that I had moaned and groaned and that I was no fucking good at all; he hoped she would straighten me up because he wasn't going to put up with my awkward ways any more. He expected his children to obey him and that it was all my mother's fault.

She straightened me up all right – hit me, kicked me, pulled me up when I fell down – every bit of my body hurt. What did I ever do to them to make them like this, it had to be all my fault, but I couldn't think why. How I hated them both, no one else ever got beaten like this. I guess she never really wanted me – well then, why didn't she give me away? I couldn't have had a worse home then that one.

The trouble was next day I would forgive her, I loved her and tried to make excuses for her behaviour and I would do anything for her, if only she'd tell me she was pleased with me for once it would have kept me going till the next beating. Well thank God it was back to work tomorrow. I seemed to be doing OK there, they were even training me to serve the customers now. I had my own little pad that I had to write down all the prices on and add it up for the customers.

My best times were down in the cellar with Joan when she would tell me stories about her family. She had two daughters and one son, her husband was a local postman. They seemed like a very nice family, but then again, my idea of a nice family would be any one where they didn't fight and beat you.

I kept on taking my pay packet home to mother unopened. One pay day I felt rebellious and opened it. I got paid £2. 7d. 6s., not a lot I suppose, but I thought it was good for Mother.

Anyway that week I took out 3d. for a Blue Ribbon biscuit to eat at break-time. I felt really good about it, quite grown up because I had opened my own pay packet. Mother went mad that evening. I didn't feel so grown up and clever then, I can tell you.

My usual routine of an evening after I had done my jobs at home was to go walking down the fields by the beck side with our little terrier. He loved it down the beck and so did I. It was my own little make-believe world down there, where no one could touch me and I could talk to anyone I wanted, and make them talk back to me. They only they said the things I wanted to hear, quite mad really.

I met Constance and Pat on one of my nightly walks, they worked at the local chicken factory and earned three times the amount that I earned. They said that I could get a job up with them as they always wanted workers. I told them that my mother would never let me go to a factory, they thought that was quite funny as their mothers never stopped them doing anything. But they laughed with me and not at me.

They said that there was a fair coming to the town next weekend and why didn't I meet them and go with them. Fat chance, no money, but I didn't want them to know that and said yes, that I would meet them on Saturday night.

Friday night soon came round again and I gave Mother my pay packet. She seemed in a good mood so I said the girl that I worked with had asked me to go to the fair with her. I couldn't tell her it was Constance and Pat because she didn't approve of them.

To my surprise she said I could go and gave me ten shillings. to go with, but told me I must be in by 10 p.m., was I looking forward to it. I met the girls as we'd arranged and off we went. It wasn't much of a fair really, just one big roundabout, some swing boats and three stalls, but everyone thought it was good for our little town.

A boy asked me if he could take me on the roundabout, his name was Geoff, he had a speech impediment and I found it quite difficult to understand him. He was very good looking and all the girls fancied him. I wondered why he had chosen me, I was nothing special at all. Constance and Pat were better looking and better dressed and were far more grown up then I was.

Geoff was twenty years old and worked as a joiner in a small village. He owned and rode a motorbike and had a really nice smile, one that lit all his face up, but most of all he was kind and thoughtful. He asked if he could see me again; I was flattered, the problem was, of course, Mother. I felt tied to her, through fear mostly, and my commitments with the children, perhaps I would always be tied.

The only way round that was when I went for my walks, but I was worried Geoff would think I was pretty boring if I told him that's how I spent my evenings. Anyway, we arranged to meet on the Monday. I couldn't tell Mother as I knew she would go mad if I was meeting a boy. I left the fair feeling really good, the fact was someone wanted me.

Sunday was another great day, I don't think. Mother soon burst the bubble from the nice night before by telling me she was going to my grandparents for the day and I had to stay at home and look after my little sister. I didn't mind that, as she was just over a year old and very cute and lovable. She made me laugh and I could talk to her, not that she understood anything I was on about, but that didn't matter. I could be a child with her and play make-believe with her toys and dolls, she loved that. For me, make-believe was the only good part of our world, it shut out reality.

I got the housework done and the dinner prepared and spent the rest of the time playing with my little sister. Father got up washed and went to the pub as usual, saying he would see me later and his dinner had better be ready. As if I dare not have it ready and on the table with his knife and fork and sugared tea, I mention the tea as do you remember what happened when my mother once forgot to sugar it? That led to the table being upturned and her getting a good hiding.

I had to put my little sister down for her nap after her lunch, put father's lunch in the oven to keep warm till he came in, and then settled down to read for a while. But I must have fallen asleep because I woke up to find Father at his tricks with his hands on me, only this time he didn't just stop at that, he forced himself on me.

I wish I could have told someone, but I felt ashamed, guilty, embarrassed and feared that somehow it was all my fault, I didn't know how to stop him because he'd never listen to my pleading. He finally went to bed with the newspapers, but I had to go up and in the room when my sister woke up. When I did go up he was reading the newspaper and masturbating. He pulled back the covers and said get in for a while. I grabbed my sister and flew downstairs, I took her out for the afternoon knowing that by the time I returned my mother should be home and I would be safe from him.

I went to work the next day and thought about telling Joan what he was doing to me, but didn't know where to start and thought she wouldn't believe me and if she did what could she do about it. I would still have to go home and face the music. Still I would see Geoff tonight after work, and had arranged to meet him near the town. I told him that I had to be in by 10 p.m. and also that I was pretty boring really all I did on an evening was to walk with the dog. He said he was fine with that, though I was sure he could find someone more exciting.

We went for a walk through the fields and sat at the side of the water just pretty silent really as he found it difficult to communicate and I was shy anyway. He just put his arm round me and it felt good, in fact anyone that showed me the least affection seemed to be wonderful to me. I could never understand what he saw in me, I had no nice thoughts about myself at all. Geoff was a perfect gentleman and never did anything except put his arm round me and kiss me goodnight, I was pleased about that as I had enough to deal with as regards my father.

I managed to see Geoff for about a fortnight before Mother found out and said I had to stop seeing him as he was too old for me and he was backward. I tried to tell her that he wasn't, that it was just a speech impediment, but I might as well have saved my breath as she wouldn't listen. I still managed to see him for about another week and then Mother threw me out. I came in one evening and the door was locked and I could get no response. So I slept in a shed down the lane for the night – well, what sleep I could get in a cold damp shed.

I went home early the next morning and she let me in to get ready for work, but informed me that I had to stop seeing Geoff or else she would throw me out permanently and I would have nowhere to go. The next day I told him I couldn't see him any more he was devastated and said he wouldn't stop trying to see me.

For a week he rode up and down our street on his motorbike, but Mother wouldn't let me out apart from to go to work. In the end, Mother informed the police that he was pestering me and said they should have a word with him, which I guess they did because I never saw him any more. Why couldn't she let me be like a normal person with friends and nights out like other teenagers?

Things carried on pretty much as normal after that. I still got beaten up even though I was now sixteen years old; I still handed over my pay packet; Father still kept up his abuse whenever he had the chance; I still didn't know were to turn or who to talk to.

I think eventually my mind just packed it in in response to all the beatings and abuse. One morning, or so I was told – the week was totally blank to me, I was confused and troubled. I left the house at 7 a.m. although I was not expected until at work 8.30 a.m. I think I must have been in shock because when Joan arrived she could see that something obviously wasn't quite right and took me inside. I've since found out that I couldn't or wouldn't talk, I just looked blank. She put me out of the way of the bosses and set me to work. She had me putting four apples in a bag for sale; afterwards she said I had put three apples, two apples anything, but four in a bag. So, obviously I couldn't cope with that. So she set me on putting together 1lb bags of tomatoes, but she was mistaken about that as well – I couldn't do it either; bet she was relieved when it came to lunchtime.

She decided to take me home with her at lunchtime as she hadn't time to take me to my own home and said she would see my parents after work. We had no sooner set off then my brother turned up and said that he had to take me home. Joan told him that I wasn't quite with it and I would need a doctor, but did he care? I can remember him cursing at me all the way home because he had to take a day off work because of me.

When I got home Mother insisted that I help her clean the house. I was still confused and shocked from the events of the previous night because when Mother asked for something off a shelf, I kept handing her something entirely different. I was convinced that whatever it was that I was supposed to get was in my hand every time I gave it to her. All I received from her was a good belt round the head and told not to be so bloody stupid, and I kept saying that it was there in my hand and as far as I was concerned it was.

Eventually she picked up that things weren't quite right with me. My mother got the doctor out. To this day I have no idea what was wrong with me, but one week of my life was left unaccounted for.

I settled back into the routine at work and one day Fred, one of the drivers, wanted someone on the mobile grocery shop with him, so I was chosen. Fred was great fun and we went round all the little villages, it also got me out of going home at lunchtime. I did that for a week and then odd days when the other woman was unable to do it for one reason or another. I loved every minute of it, it was hard work loading the van every evening ready for next day, but I didn't mind that.

I still saw Constance and Pat, on rare occasions they would ask me to go out one evening. I would say that if I could get some money I would go. This they couldn't understand as they didn't have to give their wages to their mothers. They said once again that I should go to the factory. I asked Mother if I could go out with Maud from work one weekend, and of course she asked what we had planned. So I told her the first thing that came into my head, which was the pictures. She said as long as I was home for 10 p.m., she guessed it would be OK.

So I met the girls as arranged and for once in my life never thought about what I was doing and even though I was underage for the pubs I quickly let the girls talk me into going. I had never had a drink in my life so I didn't know what I wanted, fortunately the girls sorted all that out. Well, it was inevitable that I was soon worse for wear and reached the stage where I was getting worried about returning home. It was thirty minutes past the hour I should have been home, and it would be another hour before I got home. I only hoped Mother had gone to bed early and wouldn't hear me come in.

I got near home and who should be walking to meet me, but my mother. When she got near me, she grabbed hold of me and accused me of being with a boy, she said that she had seen him step back in the shadows as she approached me. My denial just didn't reach her; she was convinced she was right. Then she smelt the drink and cigarettes, did I get a good beating for that stunt. Never pulled that one again, I can tell you.

The next day I went to work as normal and the day was going quite well until I had to collect some goods from the shelves at the back. The sack barrow that we used was behind some stock, as I lifted it out to get to the shelf, it slipped out of my hands and landed on my toes; boy, that made me shout out! I only had soft shoes on, but carried on working until Joan saw my foot. There was blood on my shoe and on its removal you could see that I had split one of my toes. I knew it hurt, but didn't think that it was that bad till it was examined. Joan had a word with the manager and she was told to take me to the local hospital. There they strapped it up and told me to go home and rest it and return for a clean dressing. I thought it a lot of fuss about nothing and I didn't want to go home, but I had very little choice in the matter.

I went home as ordered, and was Mother concerned? Of course not, she let me have the rest of the day off, but the next morning I had to help her with the housework and the kids, she said that if I wasn't earning then I had to work for my keep. So really nothing was any different.

I met the girls a couple of days later and they started on about the factory again. I told them I was on the sick at the moment and they said that now would be a good time to apply for a job with them. I must admit that the extra money sure sounded tempting and there was no way that Mother could take *that* much off me.

Anyway I went behind her back on my last day off work and had an interview. I was told that I could start on the Monday, but I had to let them know if I wanted the job by the Friday before. They gave me all the details about the pick-up points of the bus and the canteen. They had a social club for the workers that they showed me and although some of it was not very nice, like the killing line, I was sure that I could do the job. Now the problem was how to tell Mother that I had the chance of another job. Perhaps if I talked to her and explained that it meant more money and that she would benefit from it too, she would let me take the job. Plus on my side, I would have some money in my pocket for a change.

Mother seemed to see my point of view, perhaps it was the fact that she would be better off. I went up to my old job and told them that I would not be returning as I had a better job. I would miss Joan, but she said that I had to keep in touch and was always welcome at her home. I thought that was really nice, it goes to show that there are some nice people in the world and I just hadn't met many.

Well, Monday came and I walked down to the bus with the girls. I was very nervous about starting a new job, but the girls were a right laugh on the bus, we sat and had a ciggy before we got there. I had to go to the personnel office when I got there and fill in forms about ailments, next of kin and things like that. Then I got fitted out with a uniform and told all the routine things, like about the washing of the uniform. I was issued with a locker key for my spare gear then told which section I would be working in. Thank God, it wasn't the killing line.

I was placed at the packing end of the factory. It seemed very difficult at first, but I soon got the hang of it. The girls in that section seemed quite nice and I soon made new friends. The nicest one of the gang was called Shirley. She was about twenty-five years old; she lived with her mother and had a really good sense of humour. She taught me everything in the packing department, and I usually sat with her at break-times, at lunchtime we would play table tennis or listen to the juke box and just talk.

I had to work for a week without money, so had to borrow off Mother for my lunch money, and I did without lunch some days to buy my cigs, but I got by till pay day.

Mother was quite happy when I paid her as she now had an increase in the lodge money, but better than that I now had some money in my pocket for a change. I didn't quite know what to do with it, but it felt good.

The second time I got paid I bought the kids a toy each, you should have seen their faces, they lit up. Another time I bought her some chocolates, but all she managed to say to me was thanks, couldn't she have at least been happier about the present? One night I took her out to the pictures as I knew she wanted to see this particular film. My big brother looked after the children and Father as usual went to the pub. After we left the picture house as we were walking home my father came walking up the street I figured he was just being nice and had come to meet my mother, how wrong can you be?

He grabbed hold of her and gave her a slap. He said that we had not been to the pictures, but that my mother had been seeing another man and I had just been covering up for her. As much as I tried to tell him otherwise, he wouldn't have it. He dragged her home, cursing her all the way and when we got there I had to watch him beat her. *Why can't we just be a normal family?*

He finally gave up and went to bed leaving my mother crying her eyes out. I tried to comfort her, but didn't feel like I was getting anywhere.

She eventually went off to bed. I found it very difficult to understand how she could sleep next to him after the beating he had just given her. It certainly spoilt that night out.

VII

The weeks went by and I was now a part of the factory gang. Most weeks I would buy my mother a present; all I wanted to do was make her love me, but whatever I gave her made no difference to the way she treated me or her feeling towards me. I still had to cope with Father's sexual abuse and, between it all, I knew that I had to find some solution, some way out.

The only thing that I could come up with was to end my life and escape everything completely.

Mother had some sleeping tablets that she took occasionally. I thought that I had it all planned pretty well. I took the tablets with me to work and figured out that if I took them at lunchtime by the time the bus came that night I would be able to get off down by the fields which I loved and that would be the end of me. I wasn't in the least bit afraid of dying, in fact it would be a relief; no one would miss me, except maybe the children, but even they were growing up and no longer seemed to need me as much.

Bad calculations I'm afraid, by mid-afternoon I started to feel sleepy. I thought perhaps I could go off to the toilet block and lock myself in and no one would find me till it was too late. The trouble was Shirley – she noticed something wasn't quite right and asked the supervisor if she could take me to the sick bay. On the way out of the factory I asked her just to leave me and I would go home, there was no need to take me to the sick bay. I didn't fool her one bit and she asked me what I had taken. I told her I just wanted to die and asked her to please leave me. She asked me why I wanted to die and I told her about my father. What did it matter now as I was going.

Well as you might have guessed I came round lying in a hospital bed with the police at my side, asking me how long my father had been abusing me. I couldn't work out at first how they knew, but then realised I had spoken to Shirley. She must have told them. Now what was I going to do? It had all gone terribly wrong, not like I had planned at all.

The police kept on at me to tell them. Eventually I told them, I didn't care any more what happened or what my mother did when I got home, I only knew that I was at the end. The police were very persistent and they wanted to know every little detail about what went on with my father and when I say detail I mean *detail*. I found it very distressing going over it all. They then said that they would send a doctor to examine me. I never want to go through an examination like that again, it was awfully embarrassing. The humiliation – I felt like I was the one that had done wrong, maybe I was.

Next thing that I knew, a social worker was there at the side of my bed, telling me that I would not be going home at the present, but that they would be taking me to a foster home and that my parents would not be able to see me. I felt unsure about what was to happen to me or my job, and there were mixed emotions going through my head. Would I ever see my brothers and little sister again? I didn't dare question anything; I just went along with whatever they said.

The police were back the next day with more questions and said that the doctor had confirmed that I had had sex; they asked if I was sure it had been with my father and not my boyfriend. I found out later that the boy who lived over the road had said that he had had sex with me. Why on earth he would say that I don't know, I can only surmise that my father paid him to make a statement like that because I had never even been friends with him. I thought the police didn't believe me, or that's how they made me feel. The hospital said they saw no reason to keep me there so I could go the next day.

The social worker came back and told me she would pick me up and take me shopping for clothes before she took me to my foster home. I couldn't understand why they had to buy me clothes when I had them all at home. What I didn't realise was that my mother wouldn't give them to me.

The next morning the social worker came as promised and took me shopping. She was really nice and didn't question me about anything, just talked to me like a human being. She told me I was going up to a place called Hillsdale to a couple called Mary and Cyril Dodds. Well, I didn't have a clue as to where this place was. We seemed to be on the road for ages and arrived at a farm that seemed to be in the middle of nowhere with hills around it and nothing but wide open spaces. We went inside and there was one girl there who seemed odd to me. Later I found out that she was a hired hand that the Dodds took on because no one else wanted her as she had the mind of a ten-year-old.

Mary sent her out to chop logs and we then went through to their drawing room with cups of tea; she seemed like a nice caring woman. They explained to me that I would not go home, but would live with her and her husband as one of the family for a while. The social worker told her that I smoked and said that they would give me pocket money to pay for personal things and my cigarettes. Why would they do all this, I asked myself, after all, I was a complete stranger to them.

Mary said that she would show me to my room and I could unpack my things while she had a chat to the social worker. The room seemed strange to me and it certainly was cold there. They had told me to come down when I was ready, so I returned to the room. My social worker said that she would see me in two days, as that was when the police were coming back to see me again. Mary said that she had to get the supper for the menfolk, but I could have a walk round the place if I wanted. I went outside to find a pig strung up in a shed and two men who were cutting it all up. I felt sick after seeing this as I didn't understand that the life I had come to was totally different to the one I had known. Three men came in the house to eat. Mary explained that two of them were farm hands and the third one was Cyril, her husband, and that soon her two girls would be in from school. She also told the men that I would be staying with them for a while as my parents needed a break. I was pleased she didn't tell them about my father, as I felt that it was all my fault the way things were.

Her girls were twelve and fourteen years old and really made me feel at home. They showed me their rooms and their things and said that if I wanted anything I just had to ask them, then they took me out in the farmyard and showed me around the animals –geese, cows and things.

The kindness shown to me by complete strangers plus the different kind of lifestyle was all too much to take in. I couldn't quite understand that my parents couldn't touch me and that I was safe there. I asked if it was all right if I went to bed as I was very tired, Mary said that I didn't have to ask to go to bed, it was my room and I could go to it any time I wanted, but just to say goodnight to everyone if I was going to bed. The bedroom seemed very cold and I didn't think I would get to sleep after all that had happened. But soon I did. I had forgotten to turn the light off. It was still on the next morning when I got up and I felt sure I was starting the day off on the wrong foot, but when I went down, nothing was said.

I sat down to breakfast and even that was strange to me. It consisted of fatty bacon and dry bread and a big teapot full of tea; everyone seemed to be enjoying it. My first taste of this meal and I thought it was disgusting, but maybe this was just one meal and we would have something different tomorrow. I ate a little bit because I was hungry, the men then went their separate ways to work on the farm. I didn't know that they had already been out and done work before everyone else had got out of bed, but did wonder why they had come in from outside to eat. I asked Mary if she wanted a hand to wash up and she seemed quite surprised, she said that I didn't have to do anything that I didn't want to do.

Becky the backward girl didn't seem very friendly, but I found out much later that she didn't like outsiders doing what she thought were her tasks. I told her that I didn't want to stand on anyone's toes and I would fit in with whatever she wanted. That seemed to alter her face and she even chatted. The other problem I had was trying to understand everyone, as when they talked as it was in very broad Yorkshire accent, which may as well have been a foreign language to me.

Lunchtime and, guess what, fatty bacon, mashed spuds and a big pot of tea. The only thing that changed was that of an evening we had scones and cakes, all homemade that Mary had made. It was the same every day except Sunday or when we had visitors like the man from social services or Mary and Cyril's friends. But I soon got used to it and ate well like everyone else, in fact Mary used to joke with the social services about how well I ate.

I went to bed that night with the thought of the police coming again the next day. If only they sounded as if they believed me and didn't go over everything in great detail. I found it humiliating and embarrassing as they wanted to know every detail, such has were had he touched me, what position I was in, where he put his penis and everything else connected to the abuse.

I was quite surprised at Mary, because she said, of course I was telling the truth, and that no one could possibly invent such a story in such detail over and over again. The police said that owing to the boy's statement and my father's denial and my mother saying that I had always invented tales, they had no proof to convict my father, but that the case would stay open on the chance that he would assault someone else and then it would all be brought up against him.

So I figured that I would soon have to go home to face them. Mary said that I would stop there as long as possible and I need not be afraid of anyone finding out where I was. I went to bed at night feeling quite safe, but still leaving the light on. Eventually Mary asked why I left the light on all night. I thought she was going to have a go at me when I told her I was scared of the dark; all she said was that that was fine if I felt happier with it on.

It was a great life. Some days I would go out with Mary shopping, other days I would help her round the place and she always appreciated it when I helped her. I can remember one occasion she had gone out and asked Barbara to give the kitchen a good clean so I told Barbara that I would help her if she wanted me to, so we set off cleaning and when Mary returned she said that she could see that I had done some of it because it looked marvellous and gave me lots of praise – so different from my mother. That made me feel really good – the thanks and the praise were better than if I had been given a big present.

I spent a lot of my time with a book up in the hills among the heather; no one questioned me or told me off for going out all day.

If I was feeling upset or angry for no reason I would take myself off to the woodshed and chop a great pile of logs. I had also made it my job to get the ducks and geese in every evening, I enjoyed doing things because I always got thanked and praised for the things I did. When Mary and the family went out to their friends at Fairdale they always took me with them and made me feel like their own family. Nothing was heard from my home, but I often wondered how my brothers and sisters were doing, and if my mother was OK. I missed them, but didn't miss the beatings and feelings of insecurity.

For once in my life I was very happy, I felt loved and secure with the Dodds and I must admit I was beginning to love them too. But there was now talk of me going out to work. My social worker told me she had found a job for me as a maid in a public house at Osmotherly about twelve miles from Mary's and asked me how I felt about living in there. Well, if I was to be truthful, I never wanted to leave Mary's, but I did understand that they could not keep me for ever and that I would have to earn my own wages so I went along with it.

Both Mary and the social worker took me down to the pub. The owners didn't seem too bad, it just seemed strange having another home again, I still missed my family and wondered how they all were. I worried about Mother, not being there for her when she got beaten, as no doubt *he* hadn't changed.

I moved into my new job and was told what my duties were. They were to light the fires around the place at 7 a.m., to clean the bar after the night, and again before and after lunchtime opening. The rest of the time I have to clean the private areas and prepare veg and things for meals. I had one day off a week and if I went away, I had to be back by early morning to light the fires. Mary told me before she left me that she was only a phone call away if I needed her and that she would come down and pick me up on my days off if that's what I wanted.

So my life settled down to cleaning and my days off were spent with Mary and family, she wouldn't let me do anything on my days off so most of the time I spent on the hills. Usually I would sleep over and Mary would take me back next morning.

One time after my day off we arrived back thirty minutes late. The woman was fine with Mary, but after she had gone I was told that if I was going to be late back that I had better stop there on my day off. That worried me as I wanted to see the Dodds on my day off. Perhaps I didn't concentrate enough on my jobs because she wasn't very happy with me for the next couple of days. One morning I got up late owing to the fact that I felt very tired the previous night and hadn't slept very well. The landlady was furious and I was scared, she seemed just like my mother and I did think I was going to get hit. I worried that I would get into trouble with the social services and that Mary wouldn't be happy with me, I was sure that I had let everyone down. I couldn't get it through my head that those days had gone and that no one would be like my mother with me.

Anyway, I went home to Hillsdale on my next day off and Mary must have known that there was something not quite right because she started questioning me and I told her that the landlady wasn't very happy with me of late. Mary said that if I wasn't happy there I needn't stay because no one had the right to treat me badly.

I returned to the pub, as I didn't want to just leave and thought maybe it had been a one-off with the landlady – I always made excuses for peoples behaviour me, and still do it. I can never think that maybe there is some bad in people and they enjoy having a go.

Things weren't too bad after that, I suppose at least she didn't beat me, but one night she was in a really bad mood and I got the blunt end of it. It seemed that everything I did that day wasn't right for her. I got pretty upset and when I talked to Mary that evening I broke down and cried, something I seldom did. To me tears were a sign of weakness, plus it had been drilled into me as a child not to be a big baby. I have never heard Mary so annoyed and she said that she was on her way down and I was to pack my things as she was taking me home with her. When she arrived she gave the landlady a good telling off and said that she would make sure that the social services never sent her anyone again as she wasn't fit to have anyone else to work for her.

So I returned back to the Dodds and my routine there. The head of social services came for lunch with my social worker and told me that they were pleased I hadn't stopped at the pub if I wasn't happy, they said that I could stop at the Dodds until they found me another position. So I settled back down to my life there, it was very simple and extremely happy. I had one little set to with Barbara whom I had upset one day. I can't remember why or how I had upset her, but she came in the woodshed where I was chopping logs and went for me with an axe. She was very strong and if Cyril hadn't come in when he did, I dare say I would have been in a hospital.

Talking about hospitals, this is exactly were I did end up one evening. I had started acting really strange and Mary phoned for an ambulance. It turned out that I had taken a fit but they seemed to think it was a one-off.

Well, the social workers managed to fix up another job for me, but before I was able to take the position I started getting phone calls from my mother. She said that she couldn't stand it any more and would I please tell the truth, that my father hadn't touched me. She said that if I didn't and didn't return home she would kill herself. Mary told me not to take any notice and couldn't understand how she had found out were I was.

Well, of course, it really ended up getting to me. She kept phoning and, even though Mary said I didn't have to talk to her, something inside me couldn't say no. My mother has always had a hold on me due to the fact that I worshipped the ground she walked on, regardless of what she had ever done to me. Strange I know, but she had that effect on me till the day she died and then all I can say is that I felt a sense of release.

The next time she phoned I told her that I would not change what I had said about my father as it was the truth, but I would return home if she wanted me to. So return I did. It might seem strange to you, going back to where I was so unhappy after I had been so happy with the Dodds, but that was the way it was with me and I could never explain it myself.

Mary said that she understood and that she would always be there if I needed her and to this very day I have kept in touch with her.

VIII

It seemed like no one at home knew why I had been away and that suited me just fine. Father never spoke to me on my return and mother was also very cool towards me, but my brothers and little sister were so happy to see me that it made up for the cool reception showed by my parents.

I applied to go back to the factory to work and they accepted me, so things soon settled down to a routine again. I was placed in a different area in the factory, but it was not on the killing line so I soon picked that job up. We had two supervisors, one was really nice and knew how to have a laugh with her workers, the other one was a bit of a misery guts and so straight-laced. Well, lucky for me I got on the nice one's line.

There were two girls with whom I had to work closely, with one was very nice and full of fun and the other one seemed to resent me; it seemed she didn't like anyone else in on their friendship. Well I didn't really care because since I had returned from the Dodds I was stronger in my mind somehow. In fact, I even dared to stand up to my mother a bit, I daren't push it too far though.

There was another girl at the factory who I won't say too much about, but we got very close and we would meet of an evening sometimes. As she lived in a small village away from me it was awkward to meet often.

I would still go through the field of an evening even though the dog was no longer with us. I was by now seventeen years of age and I still played make-believe, only most of the time it was when I went to bed. Also now that I felt my mother's control wasn't as strict, and she couldn't have everything all her own way I didn't come in at 10 p.m.. So most of the evenings I sat in a little café in town, drank coffee and made new friends there. Funny how most of my friends seemed to be older women, maybe I felt that I was always looking for a mother figure and I was certainly always looking for approval.

My new friend from the factory came down twice a week and we would sit and talk. She wasn't particularly attractive, but somehow I felt drawn to her, it frightened me a bit the way I felt. We would walk down the fields and just sit with our arms around each other. The thing was I knew that I wanted to be closer, but didn't know how and was too scared of the way I felt to get closer.

I came in one night late and Mother gave me a beating; I was still too scared to answer back on that score. Father hadn't altered as regards beating Mother up. One night after he had hit her he went upstairs. My two brothers slept in a big bed in my elder brother's room, he threw the bed over on top of the boys who were aged six and five and left them crying and confused as they didn't know what was happening to them. Mother came rushing up the stairs and grabbed the boys and we all locked ourselves in the bathroom. Father broke down the bathroom door and started again. The thing that broke me up was when the six-year-old cried and said 'Please don't hit Mammy,' so Father gave him a slap also, what a bloody pig he was. It seemed like he was using the boys to hurt my mother, and it worked, because although she didn't love me she worshipped the other children. Although Father never had stopped abusing me, there were still the suggestions and the little gibes, like the fact that he had got away with it and my word stood for nothing.

Things at work were going OK at the moment and all in all I suppose my life wasn't too bad. I phoned Mary a lot and worked out when I was going up to see her. That didn't go down really well with Mother, I think she was possibly jealous because she knew that I had got very close to Mary in the time that I spent there. The fact that I even left home was never talked about, you would think it had never happened at all.

I was at work one day and came round in the nurse's room, or that sick bay, as it was called. It turned out that I had had another fit. The nurse contacted my mother and informed her and said that I should see the doctor. Well, when I got home you would have thought I had robbed a bank or something. Mother kept on saying that she didn't think I had thrown a fit and that there had never been anything in her family like that. I didn't realise that there was a stigma attached to fits then. Anyway, I went up to the doctor's and after the description given to him he said that it 'sounded like epilepsy' and he put me on a course of anti-depressants. Well, Mother threw a fit when we reached home, said that I was an embarrassment to the family and I had better stop it. As if I had any control over it.

The fits continued and the people whom I worked with knew the signs and I usually slept it off in the sick bay.

Things were getting a bit difficult at home again with Mother, her usual trick was to throw me out and I would end up sleeping wherever I could. For some reason I felt really down and just didn't want to live any more so I saved up my anti-depressants and bought tablets from the chemist. I went to the fields with some bottles. I went up to the top of a field where hardly anyone walked and took the tablets. The last thing I remember was feeling dozy and I laid down and felt really good, happy. Well, next thing I knew was waking up in a hospital bed with tubes.

I never saw Mother or anyone that I knew, but when I came round there was a doctor at my bedside and he said that a shrink would be seeing me tomorrow. That must mean I am as mad as a hatter, I guessed. Mother always said there was something wrong with me she must have been right. The shrink asked me why I had taken the tablets and I would have thought it was obvious to any fool that I wanted to die, I couldn't be bothered with anything any more and couldn't see a purpose in anything any more, I just wanted peace. He had seen my mother before seeing me and she had told him that I was normally a happy person and that she was upset because it was not the first time I had done this, but last time I had accused my father of doing things. She said that I had always been a difficult child and I was getting worse. It ended up with the shrink telling my mother that I was depressed and a course of tablets would soon get me back to normal.

I went to see Mary, but couldn't tell her what I had done because I felt like I had let her down in some way. I always let everyone down sooner or later. I just showed her the happy pretend side that I showed to everyone. They all thought I was a good laugh, the life and soul of the party – that's all I ever wanted anyone to see.

I didn't return to the factory when I came home, but got a job at a transport café. I cleared tables and washed up and spent most of the time in the back kitchen, but that suited me as I was always busy so had no time to think. I would come home of an evening and go straight out to the little café. I had finished with my friend from the factory after she had got herself a boyfriend and I couldn't really deal with that. It felt like I was the outsider looking in and couldn't work out my feelings, I was very confused.

I hadn't been working at the café for long when Mother said that my lodge money had to go up. I pleaded with her that I couldn't afford it, but all she said was that if I didn't like it I could get out. Great, where could I go? I didn't really know anyone anyway, so I turned and said that she couldn't have what I hadn't got.

Well, the outcome of that little rebellion was when I came home from work the next evening the door was locked and she told me to find somewhere else to live. I didn't know quite what to do so I walked up to the café and sat and had a coffee and played some music on the jukebox. Funny how music makes your mind go round. I decided to sleep in a shed that night, thinking perhaps something would come to me. I knew it was no good going back and pleading with my mother. I went to work the next day as usual and said nothing to anyone, just laughed and joked as usual.

The next night I managed to sleep in the local fish shop, as they had left a window open round the back. At least there was water in there and I could have a wash. As regards clothes, well, that was another matter.

I went to the café that night and one of the women there whom I had got to know quite well asked me what the matter was. Well, as usual, I thought I could put on a brave face and bluff my way out of it. I wasn't doing very well I'm afraid, as she noticed that I hadn't changed for a couple of days. I must admit that my attire was becoming a bit of a problem. I had to tell her that my mother had thrown me out and I had no clothes. Bless her, she took me home with her and said that I could stay there until I had something sorted out; as for my clothes, she had a daughter of her own and so I had a change of clothes for the next day. She said that she would go with me to the shop in town and join a club so I could get a couple of changes of clothes.

She was a canny little woman and a very good worker, her husband was a taxi driver and a very large man into the bargain, and they had a boy and a girl who were nice kids too. The next day she told me she had found me some lodgings about half a mile out of town. She said the woman had a bit of a reputation, but she was a nice enough woman. Well, I knew that she could only put me up temporarily. So time to move on and I moved into my new home. There were two teenage boys there and strangely enough I had gone to school with one of them. The mother was a bit flighty and had men on the side, but no one seemed to care or so I thought at the time.

By this time my hours of work had changed – I started at five in the morning and finished at 10 a.m. Then I'd go back at 6 p.m. and work until 10 p.m. I didn't mind that shift too much as I could have a sleep in the afternoon before I returned in the evening, so it kept my days pretty full.

One evening a young man came in and he sat there most of the evening with a coffee. He smiled when I went round clearing the tables. He seemed like a pleasant person. He started coming in about three times a week and we soon got chatting. He said his name was Barry and that he was a steelworker in Middlesbrough. He asked me out to the pictures one night and I accepted. He didn't put a hand wrong and we soon were going out together. It was hard on him because he had to come from Middlesbrough to see me, but it was nice to feel wanted and Barry certainly made me feel wanted. I always knew when he was in the café as he would put a certain record on the jukebox.

My next weekend off Barry asked me to go up home with him and meet his family. He was getting a little bit too serious for me, and yet he still never did anything out of line, just held my hand and kissed me. He made it sound attractive up in Middlesbrough so I agreed to go with him.

His mother was nice and so was his dad. He had two brothers and one sister; his sister was married, but his brothers weren't, one was in the army and the other one worked with Barry at the steelworks.

I didn't like the area where he lived, the steelworks smelled and if you wore white it got all covered in black smuts.

The next morning we got up at 5 a.m. and they said we were all going swimming. I made the excuse up that I hadn't got a costume and they said I could watch them if I wanted or I could stop at home. I didn't want to tell them that I was scared of water, but as they all swam like fishes I thought one day I would learn to swim as it looked like such fun, one day.

I saw my mother in town one day and she was really nice to me. She made out that it was me who had left home and not she who had thrown me out, said that I should come round to see my brothers and sisters as they asked after me and couldn't understand why I wasn't there. Boy, she always knew how to get to me. Anyway things were soon taken out of my hands as the lady I stayed with had a big row with her husband and she ended up stabbing him so she was taken away by the police. As it turned out he refused to press charges so she was soon released, but in the meantime I had been persuaded to return home.

I still had my job at the café, but I was getting rather sick of doing all the work while the others, who were all elderly women, seemed to do nothing. Once again I stood up for myself and went to see the owner who lived above the café and told her how I felt. She said that I was the youngest member of staff and so therefore I was meant to do twice as much work. My answer to that was I should have twice as much money at which she just laughed and told me to get back to work.

I told her in no uncertain terms where to stick her job and walked out. I never even gave a thought as to what my mother's reaction would be, and right then I really didn't care. I met Barry that night before I even saw my mother and he said that I did right to tell her what to do with the job. It's nice to have someone to stand by you.

I told mother when I got home and as you can guess she wasn't very happy with me. Then again, was she ever? I told her about Barry at the same time, I thought that I might as well get it all over with at once. Of course, what did I get but 'he would have to be a waster', 'why couldn't he find a girl from where he came from' and 'there must be something wrong with him'. No one that had anything to do with me was ever any good as far as she was concerned.

I went to the job centre the next day and there was a temporary job at a grocery shop in the town so I went to see about that and got it. I was told to start straight away, and thought that should keep Mother quiet.

The shop was managed by a family – a father, son and daughter. The father was a bit of a miserable sod and the son was about the same, but the girl was OK. A bit of a family person, she had to ask mammy and daddy for permission to do anything, but we soon became friends and she used to come out with me on an evening. We only sat in the café and played music; she would always put the same record on and then sit there looking at me. I remember the record well and realised later on in life why.

She didn't like the time that I spent with Barry and hated it even more when he wanted to get engaged, as I agreed to get engaged to him. Big mistake. Once we got engaged he wanted to take the relationship a bit further. Well I couldn't say no all the time because then he might get sick of me and leave me for someone else, but I wasn't keen on that part of the relationship at all. I guess that's what love's all about, or so I thought at that time. Anyway once the pressure of sex came into the relationship I soon got sick and eventually I finished with Barry. He was devastated and kept showing up to try and make me change my mind. The relationship was on and off like I don't know what.

My new friend was always very happy when I had sent Barry packing and of course my mother said that she knew it wouldn't last. I must give Barry ten out of ten for his persistence because he never gave up on me.

My brothers and sisters were growing up, but still relied on me for things like bonfire night when mother would forget or just refuse to buy fireworks. I can always remember how it felt when I couldn't have any, and I didn't want them to feel like that so I used to make a bonfire and buy fireworks for them. Mother used to say that it was a waste of money, but I knew they felt good and enjoyed it and that brought me pleasure. If ever I had any extra money I would buy Mother presents but she never appreciated them. I was still looking for some love, or for anything, I guess.

The job finished at the grocery shop, well I knew it wasn't permanent. The dole office didn't have anything in so I ended going back to the chicken factory, and got my old job back on the trussing line. The same girls were there that I worked with before, so things soon settled down into the same routine again.

We still went round the fields and to the café and odd times we went to the pictures. Barry and I weren't together at that time, in fact I was asked out by a boy in the factory. His name was Sam, he was very good looking and it made me feel good as all the girls were after him and I had him. He had a car so we would go out for a drink into the country and up to the coast and different places of a weekend. It all went pretty well until sex reared its ugly head and then I didn't want to know. One night we had a big row in the country and I got out of the car to walk home. He couldn't understand it, he said that all the girls he had been out with had only been interested in what he had to offer in that department.

We didn't finish over it, in fact I think he got the message for a while, but only for a while. Then he said that there was something wrong with me because I wasn't interested in sex. Maybe he was right, maybe there was something wrong, we finished on that note in any case.

I couldn't believe it when my mother got pregnant again. I thought she was too old to have any more as she was forty years old by that point and who has kids then?

I was feeling depressed again and had to make a visit to the doctor's. He gave me tablets again only this time they didn't seem to be working and I had the most strange feelings when I walked. It felt like I was floating and when people spoke to me it seemed as if their voices were distant and far away. I was signed off work and didn't feel as if I could cope with things, I ended up going to see a shrink again as an outpatient in the local hospital. I told him about the strange feelings, but when it came to anything else I couldn't talk to him. He changed my tablets, but owing to my past record they were given out to me under supervision at home. When I returned to work the nurse had them and I had to go to her twice a day for my pill. The nurse was lovely and we had a laugh. She seemed very understanding and when I played my make-believe games at night, it was usually her I talked to.

Things were not very nice at work at that time as I worked opposite a girl whose friend had a white coat charge hands position in the factory and that gave her power over me. Because she was jealous of the way her friend and I got on, she started picking on me. She managed to make the other three girls that I worked near do nothing, but sing this stupid song all day long. I can still remember the song to this day and still hate it as much: 'I'm H–A–P–P–Y all day and send me to Coventry.'

Well, I couldn't take it and must have snapped. I don't remember, but was told later that, as we were going for our breaks, I went into the sick bay came out with a pair of scissors and knifed this charge hand under her eye. I came round in the hospital wondering why I was there. I can't ever remember anyone telling me what the problem was with me.

Of course it goes without saying that I lost my job, so once more I joined the ranks of the unemployed. This came in handy for Mother, I suppose with her being pregnant, as she wasn't carrying this one very well.

Mother seemed quite pleased to have me home and for once we seemed to get on well, one day at a time. Anyway there was only my little sister at home at that time as the other two were at school. I used to take them to school in the morning and collect them of an evening, Mother didn't go out very much at all so all the shopping and things were left to me. But for once I felt as if I was being useful and needed, if it was only for the work.

I didn't have much money as my only income was from the dole and Mother wanted most of that. She had got rid of most of the baby things thinking that she wouldn't have any more and as usual Father wouldn't part with any extra money.

The doctors had decided that Mother had to go into hospital to have this baby owing to her age, and I had no choice but to look after everything when she went in. I still went to the café at night as it was my only break from home, and I was still on the tablets, but Mother was too busy to supervise me with them so I was trusted to take them.

Barry still came round the town to see if I was around and on the odd occasion we would go out together to the pictures or just for a walk. I must admit that he really cared about me and I almost felt sorry for him as I didn't think that I was capable of loving anyone except my family who could not love me.

Father was being his usual rotten self and, though he didn't hit my mother through this pregnancy, he would get to her with the things he did, like trashing the house and verbal abuse which was just as bad as the beatings. Believe me, no one knew that better than me; it was Mother's favourite tool towards me those days. The trouble with words was that they ate at you in your mind and you could never get rid of them. It was a bit like a disease that you could never cut out.

The time soon came round for Mother to go into hospital to have the baby. The hospital was about nine miles away and the bus service was very good so after she had given birth to another boy, I got my auntie to look after the kids and went to see her.

I was twenty years old by this time and rumour had it that this was my child. In fact, later on in my life, I had to take his birth certificate to work to prove that he wasn't my child. I wish he had been mine because then he would have been something of mine that no one could take away from me and he would love me as I was.

My new brother was wonderful and although I loved the others I idolised him. Nothing was too much trouble for me as regards him. Father tried it on while Mother was in hospital. He had gone to bed after lunch with the papers and the boys wanted to know what was on the television so I went up to the room to get a paper and it was like in the old days with the invite to join him in bed. Things were different now, I knew that Mary was there for me and she would believe me so I told him to get lost and said that I was taking the children out, which shows I didn't feel that safe really.

What's wrong with men? Are they all alike and think of nothing else but sex? Or is it something about me?

One day one of Father's friends offered me a lift to see Mother in hospital as his wife had just given birth. He was only a young man and on the way home he suggested that we go for a drink and then we could have a good time with no one finding out. I was disgusted, but at least he took my answer well, it could have been worse. But how could someone do it when the person they love has just given them a child?

Mother soon came home and I had to think about getting back to work – as she reminded me. The trouble was there weren't many jobs about so I was still at home. I loved being with my new brother, I fed him, changed him, in fact, I did most things for him. You would have thought he was mine as Mother didn't seem to be that bothered about him.

I had to go to the doctor's and get my tablets as I wasn't feeling too good again. The hassle of not having a job was getting to me and being stuck at home with Mother didn't help as she always put me down. No matter what I did, it wasn't right for her.

I didn't have any money, but I wanted to see Mary so I told Mother that I was going up there for the day, and that went down really well I can tell you. She said that if I went not to bother coming home again. Right then, I didn't care. I walked as far as Hawnby and then phoned Mary to tell her were I was. She went mad and said that I shouldn't have walked all that way and should have phoned her because she would have come for me. We went out shopping and she asked me how things were at home. I told her about my new brother but didn't tell her what things were really like. I didn't want her to feel responsible for me. I know now that she wouldn't have minded, but all through my life I have never let anyone get close enough to me to really know me. That way they can't hurt you or so I thought. I was always the fool, joking and laughing so no one could ever see the hurt or thoughts that were underneath all that.

Mary brought me back to town at the end of the day. I got her to drop me there and said I was meeting some friends, as I didn't want her to know what Mother had said to me before I left. I had hoped she had forgotten and that I could get in when I reached home.

Wishful thinking on my behalf. The door was locked and I had to think where to sleep for the night. I went up to the café, but couldn't face telling them that I was homeless again; no one could understand why I kept going home all the time, only I knew the reason. I went home at the end of the night on the off chance that my brother had come in and left the door open – this time it paid off. I climbed the stairs very quietly and crawled into bed hoping Mother would be OK in the morning.

I got up very early before anyone and lit the fire and made a pot of tea. When I heard Mother getting up I thought that it might work if she came down to the fire lit and could just sit and have a cup of tea. What did she say, but 'I thought I had told you not to come back!' I told her that I had nowhere else to go and she said, 'What a shame, because you're not staying here.' What she should have said was that she didn't want me full stop.

Anyway, the subject was soon dropped with the arrival of my brothers who had to get ready for school. I figured out that if I made myself really useful all day that she would forget what she had said, so I took the boys to school, washed and dressed my baby brother and worked hard all day helping her. Nothing else was said on that day about me leaving. The only thing that she said was the fact that she couldn't afford to keep me and it was time I started paying her back for all the years she had brought me up. I told her that I was doing my best to find a job. I was told that I was bloody useless, 'no one else seemed to have a problem'.

I overdosed again. It seemed like all I wanted to do was die, like I had a death wish. Something just came over me and I couldn't explain why I did it.

I woke up in hospital again. Mother came; she asked me to go into another hospital and told me that they would make me better. I nearly thought she cared that time, but I think the real truth was that she just wanted to get rid of the daughter who kept showing her up by trying to kill herself. The shrink came to see me and by the time he and my mother had finished I agreed to go into his hospital. It was in Middlesbrough, which would please Barry, as he was just down the road from the hospital.

They soon shipped me out to the mental hospital. I didn't know what to expect, but right then I didn't much care. All I knew was that Mother cared enough to ask me to go in there and promised me that I would be better when I came out.

In the mental hospital there was a glass office in the middle of two wards so they could see everything that happened, you had to get a key from the office to take a bath and everything you took in with you was checked. The patients did the cleaning and set the tables for every meal, all the cutlery was counted before each meal and after each meal.

You had to be supervised when you cleaned your teeth, I found out at a later date that it was in case you tried to choke yourself with the toothbrush. Some of the patients had liquid medicine and they were all stood over until it was swallowed, as they could tip it on their dinners to dispose of it. After you took your tablets you had to open your mouth and lift your tongue up so they could make sure that you had actually swallowed them.

People were there for different reasons and unless they wanted to talk no one asked why. I remember one old girl – well she seemed old to me, but now I guess she would be about thirty-five years old. Her name was Martha and all she did all day and night was to wander up and down to the door, which of course was permanently locked. I found out that she had been admitted with depression and, on her release, her father died, and she couldn't cope with it. She was in there for the rest of her life even though she had inherited her father's farm and was a wealthy woman. The hospital took care of her money; it was very sad because all she wanted to do was to go home and she never would. I used to walk up and down with her, not that she understood, but I thought she might feel better knowing that someone cared about her.

Another girl was so thin that they had to make her eat every two hours; she was a student and just forgot to eat. She had to be photographed every week, I wouldn't like that but she didn't seem to mind as she said she could see the difference each week.

Myself, well I had to take tablets every day and talk to the shrink once a week, I didn't know what good that did as I felt I could fool him quite easily.

There have always been very few people that I could really talk to in my life. Because I didn't want to be put down or judged I would keep my inner feelings to myself. After all, if I thought it was quite mad to play make-believe games at my age and want to die for no real reason, how was anyone else supposed to understand it?

Every day we had to go down to occupational therapy and make stupid baskets or knit or sew. I didn't see the point in that so I asked if I had to go, and of course you had to go every day except weekends. It was a mixed session as the men came over from their unit at the other side of the hospital and there was a lad called Tom. He was nice; I found out that he was in because he was a drug addict. He couldn't see the point in this basket weaving or anything else that they did either. We soon found out that it was OK if we played draughts all afternoon as that was considered to occupy our minds; I soon became one of the best draughts players there. It's not very interesting really, but in there it was something.

After you had been in there a while you were trusted to have your own room. It had a glass porthole in the door so that they could check on you, but was a lot more private than the wards. They never trusted you enough to have access to a bath key though. Tom and I got quite close, which was understandable seeing that we spent four hours every afternoon together, and he told me that soon they would let me out to do shopping or go for a walk and would I consider going out with him as in a relationship.

Barry still came to see me and talked about marriage when I got out of the hospital. It was a bit too serious for me so eventually I told him that we had finished and that I had met someone else.

I remember one particular day when I felt really frustrated with everything; all I wanted to do was kick something or hit something. In the end I was on washing up duty and just threw this milk bottle into the backyard. I felt better after, but not that good. The staff made me pick every bit up and I had to sit there and piece it all together. There was one small piece missing and I spent most of the night looking for it, never did find it. They thought I may have kept a piece of the milk bottle to cut my wrists.

I had soon been there two months and no one came to see me from home; I felt like I had been abandoned and perhaps I had. There was no way of me getting out as I wasn't yet twenty-one years of age and I couldn't discharge myself, so there was not a lot that I could do really. Very soon they let me out to the shops and I could have a walk round, so I would go shopping for all the other patients.

On an evening they let me out for a walk with a time restriction. It didn't take long for Tom and I to walk over to the local pub. We figured that if we drank vodka there would be no smell when we returned to the hospital. It was pretty dangerous really as I still had to go to the office for my sleeping pill when we got back. I got away with it for about two nights then went to the office for my pill only to be read the riot act about drinking and taking pills. After that they didn't let me or Tom out at night.

I went shopping one morning with the thought in my head that I wanted to get out of everything. I went to the chemist's and bought tablets. I figured that I could get some more the next day and then kill myself, so when I got back to the hospital I hid them under my mattress. When I went to bed that night the staff escorted me. It didn't dawn on me as to why, but they searched my room and of course they found the tablets. I was transferred back onto the main ward where they could watch me again.

The next day I had to see my shrink who asked me why I wanted to kill myself. I wish I could have told him why, but I didn't know myself. I just knew there was this strong feeling that I had to do it. They changed my tablets and kept a close eye on me, I wasn't allowed out any more so got pretty fed up really.

I decided to write to my mother to see if she would come and see me and get me home again, I wanted to see my baby brother – he was growing up without me, and I really missed him. I got no response to my letter at all. Why did I find that surprising: she had got rid of me at last?

One morning the sister of the ward came in and behind her was this little scraggy dog. The sister was a really nice person and I got on well with her. She said the dog had followed her to work and she couldn't get rid of it whatever she did. It was really sweet, but in need of a bit of care and attention. The sister asked me if I would mind giving it a bath and a feed as she had to get on. She gave me the shampoo and some food for it. It was a small little bitch, brown and a little bit of white on it and very affectionate. She kept licking me as I bathed her.

The dog would follow me around all day, so the sister gave me leave to take it out for a walk. As far as I was concerned it was love at first sight. That evening the sister gave me my room back and asked if I could keep the dog with me until she could find out were it came from. I called her Peggy and she stayed with me all that week and when it came to seeing my shrink the sister told me to take Peggy in with me. I thought he would go mad, but the sister said to him that she knew it wasn't really done, but that the dog had done me the world of good and could I be allowed to keep it in the hospital.

He agreed under certain conditions. I had to get it checked over at the vets and make sure it had its vaccinations. I thought that would be that. I only had my sick pay so it would be impossible. I left the room in a bad way, thinking my dog had to go, but sister followed me and told me that the shrink had agreed to the vets fees coming out of the hospital kitty. She made me an appointment at the vet for tomorrow.

I was on cloud nine. Peggy was mine all mine, no one could ever take her off me and I could love her and she could love me.

Time moved on. I still saw Tom and he wanted to get engaged so that I belonged to him and wouldn't go back to Barry. We got engaged in the hospital and the sister wasn't very happy about it. She said that she hoped I knew what I was doing as he was a drug addict and didn't I have enough problems without taking on Tom?

My friend from the grocery store wrote to me all the time I was in hospital and I found one of the letters very disturbing. She wrote that she didn't know how she was going to live without me, as her life was empty now I wasn't around and would I soon be out.

That letter went round and round in my head for days. In the end I decided to show it to the sister. She said that it sounded like my friend was a lesbian and that was the last thing I wanted. She instructed me to ignore the letter. Lesbian? What could one say? I knew that I had feelings for women that I shouldn't have, as it wasn't normal, truthfully I couldn't say that the way she felt was nothing to do with me nor that I didn't feel the same about her, so I choose to take the sister's advice and just ignore the letter.

I spent my days taking Peggy for walks, seeing Tom and going to the shops for the patients. I wondered how much longer I was going to be in there as I seemed OK now. I talked to Tom about it as he was to be discharged soon. I felt like I would be stuck in there for ever. He said that the best thing to do was go home for the day and just jump on the bus. The hospital wouldn't miss me for a few hours because I was always out with my dog, he said that he would come with me.

The next day that's exactly what we did. We got to my house where my mother was hanging the washing out, and she greeted me as if I had just being up the town shopping. She didn't act as if I had been away for nearly six months. In fact we both got a very warm welcome, she even seemed to like Tom – though no doubt that would change – and asked whose dog it was. When I told her it was mine she asked me what I was going to do with her when I came home. I told her that I would bring her home with me, which didn't go down well at first, but then she realised Tom was there and she didn't want anyone to see how she really was.

I asked her to get in touch with the hospital so that I could come home. It was lovely seeing my baby brother. He was now six months old and I had missed all that, but he gave me a lovely cuddle. I had to leave, I couldn't stop for too long as I didn't want to get into trouble when I got back to the hospital. I had to tell them where I had been because I was hopeful my mother would be getting in touch with them.

My mother did contact the hospital and they agreed for me to go home on a weekend visit. I couldn't understand why they couldn't let me go straight home, but they said that I needed to adjust to being out in the world again. I told Tom that I would look for lodgings for him while I was at home as he wanted to come home with me when he left.

The weekend was a disaster. It seemed strange being at home. I felt on edge all the time and strange away from the safety of the hospital. I couldn't cope. I ended up returning to the hospital early.

They said that it was quite normal for me to think that I would never get home, but after a few weekend visits I would OK. And sure enough within a few weeks of going home for the weekend they discharged me. Free at last!

X

We soon found a place for Tom to lodge when he got out and a job for myself in a store in the town. Things seemed to have settled down into a routine again, except now it was slightly different as I had Peggy.

Mother let me keep her with me in my room at first then she said that she had to have a kennel in the yard while I was at work because she got under Mother's feet. That I could understand, but when she said that she would have to live in the kennel all the time I wasn't very happy. However, there was not a lot I could do.

As soon as I came in from work I would give her a biscuit, get my tea and then take her for a walk. Tom was now out as well and working so we would go down the fields together. It wasn't long before he wanted to take the relationship to a sexual level, he said that we had known each other long enough. It's funny how much I changed as soon as sex came into it. I certainly didn't enjoy it, but it was the normal and accepted thing to do, wasn't it?

I spent a lot of time with the baby as well. I think that was why I put up with sex, because it was the only way to get pregnant and I really wanted our own child. It was a great longing, but I did start to wonder if perhaps I couldn't have children. Constance and Pat were both married with children and they seemed very happy.

The baby and I were very close, he would come to me or look at me before he would go to his mother.

Pretty soon Mother started telling me that I had to get rid of Peggy. I said no way, if she went then so did I, which was a rather silly statement as we both knew that it was difficult enough getting somewhere for me on my own. Getting somewhere where they allowed dogs would be impossible, but I loved my dog and I didn't care, she wasn't going. The next night I came home from work and went straight down to the kennel. Peggy didn't jump out straight away to see me as she usually did, she was all curled up as if she was fast asleep 'Come on, girl,' I called. No movement, I put my hand on her. She was stiff and cold. I screamed and Mother came out, she told me that she was dead, but that she had been all right earlier. I didn't trust her and when I went into the washhouse and it stank of gas. The window was open, and the window was never opened in the washhouse. I took Peggy out in my arms, her kennel smelt of gas as well.

I flew at my mother and told her that she had gassed my dog, *how could she?* Tom came over and he agreed that the dog had been killed, he said that he would phone the RSPCA and I hoped they would lock my mother up. It was one time in my life when I really hated her. When the authorities came and had words with my mother, she turned the water works on and was so convincing that in the end all they did was give her a warning.

I never forgave her for taking my dog from me. Peggy was something I loved and that wasn't allowed as far as she was concerned.

All my emotions afterward I channelled into my little baby brother, in fact he ended up calling me mammy, but she soon put a stop to that. Tom started back on the drugs and ended back in the hospital. He wrote, but my mother would open his letters, it was only by accident that I received one. She used to open all my mail and then get the kids to scribble on the back of the envelopes and said that they had messed with the mail.

Another thing she used to do was get the kids all ready for a trip to the seaside and then make out that I had upset her and tell them she wasn't going. She would keep that up for about an hour before the trip and then she would play the matter and say we were to go even though she was upset.

I went to see Tom in hospital, it was quite nice seeing everyone again, but I was pleased that I wasn't in there. Martha was still there padding up and down. She ended her life in there possibly thinking no one cared about her, it's a pity she couldn't have gone home.

Tom told me that he had told Esther – one of the girls that was in when I was – that he was going to be a father and we were going to get married. I guess I didn't realise how important I was to him, that like me he wanted something of his own. I knew it was no good as it wasn't what I wanted. But I played along with his little game as it seemed to make him happy. I always wanted to please everyone. I supported him while he was in the hospital, but knew that I didn't love him. Maybe I was incapable of loving anyone except my mother and sisters and brothers, maybe I'd never make love with anyone.

I finished with Tom as soon as I found out that he was due out of the hospital and told him that I couldn't make-believe with him. He came back to the town and I worried for so long, but he was soon back in the hospital.

Life went on and Mother still played her games, but now she knew that it didn't make any difference if she beat me as she couldn't hurt me like that any more so she changed her tactics and used my little brother. He was very close to me and if she upset him he used to come to me for comfort and then she would pull him out of my arms and remind me he was her child not mine. If he had been mine he wouldn't have been upset in the first place.

If he wanted something he would tell her that if she wouldn't give it to him, I would. He was right – whatever he wanted he got from me. One time I had bought him a little army wagon with soldiers in the back and he was sat on the back porch playing. Mother was in the washhouse, I had upset her over God knows what, well she stormed out and on the way kicked his toy. He got upset and ran to me, she then took his toy and broke it on the step saying that he was her child and I should mind my own business. My little brother was heartbroken and because she knew that upset me she had won again. I told him later that I would get him a new toy. When I next got paid I bought something for everyone, including my mother, but the only people who were happy were my brothers and sisters. What did I expect, my mother had never been grateful before, so why would she start now?

Barry started coming round again, saying that he couldn't forget me and wanted to go out with me again. Better the devil you know, I suppose. We got engaged again. *Maybe this is the answer, to get away from home and have my own family*. The trouble was I didn't really like sex; it was just a means to an end to get a baby of my own.

Once mother found out that I was seeing Barry again she said that I could get out. She knew that lodgings were hard to find, but she didn't care. She also knew what my brother and sister meant to me, and they got upset because they knew I would be leaving. I told my sister I would come to school during playtime to see her, but the little one, well, what could I tell him?

A women that worked at the café where I still went of an evening said that I could move in with her and her husband which I did. My room was lovely but even though they made me feel at home I felt that they were above me and so I felt uncomfortable really. She was a German lady and had come across to England after marrying during the war. She still ran down to the cellar when the fire bell went in the town, she said she thought it was an air raid warning. Her husband did something in the motor business, though I was never quite sure what. She said that they had two children, but they lived abroad. To this day neither I nor anyone else have ever seen these children, it seems like she invented them. But then we all have our own make-believe and it was very sad and she must have felt disturbed somehow that she had to invent children.

At least she had a good sense of humour and we got on well together, her husband was a really nice chap. We painted the outside wall and she said we should put a bill in for it. When he came in we presented him with our bills, he laughed and said he would have to do an inspection, he then paid us! It was all a great joke. They treated me really well and we did all sorts together. They even took me with them when they went to their friends. I did miss my family and went to see my sister at school and managed to spend a little time with her before my mother found out.

The next time I went to see my sister I was told by the teachers that they had strict instructions from my mother that I was not allowed to go near my sister. I asked them when she had given those instructions and they said about ten minutes ago. It didn't take much working out that she had gone up the town so off I went to find her, *how could she do that to me?*

I saw the pushchair outside the supermarket and knew my mother was inside. I just lost it. When she came out and I confronted her. I asked her how she could call herself a mother, what mother stops her daughter seeing her own sister. I slapped her face, something I am not proud of. I ran down the nearest alley and cried my eyes out.

Barry and I were still together and he kept talking about getting married. *Why not?* I asked myself, then I could have my own home and family and no one could interfere. I told him I would think about it and let him know soon. I knew what my answer was, but also knew that I was being very unfair to Barry, using him to get away from everything. It's just that I knew he would be good to me and hoped eventually that I could love him as he deserved and be good to him.

So the decision was made to get married some time in the near future. Barry was over the moon about it; me, I just hoped I could live up to his expectations.

The lady whom I lodged with was OK about Barry and all the women from the café said they would help to organise it for me, but I didn't want to rush into it. Before long I hit one of my depressive moods. Sometimes I realised what was happening and other times it just hit me and I just overdosed there and then. I didn't have anything to be depressed about, just felt this great urge to kill myself. I hoped that it would pass without seeing anyone. These days if I realise what is going on I know different, but back then no one seemed to understand it, least of all me. So I carried on working and going out to the café of an evening. I must admit that I didn't go out as much as I used to since moving in.

I saw Barry three nights a week and spent most weekends at Middlesbrough at his parents' house. I got on very well with them and they seemed very happy that he was going to settle down with me.

I felt this desperate urge to see Mother and my brothers and sister, but didn't know what her reaction would be as the last time I had seen her I'd hit her. I decided to take the bull by the horns and walk down there to see them all. I went when I knew the kids would be there and my father would be at the pub – I never had any urge to see him, in fact the less I saw him the better. The reception that I got from Mother was very cool to say the least, but my brothers and sister made up for her and were all so happy to see me. *Why does she have to cut me off from them? They don't understand why I can't see them and I can't explain it to them.* I think it was only the fact that I took my mother some cigarettes that she let me in in the first place.

I told her that I was planning to marry Barry. That went down really well as she never liked him in the first place. She said she wouldn't come to the wedding and didn't want to know anything about it. The kids went off to play with the toys I had brought them, which left just me and Mother and she didn't seem to want my company so I decided to leave. I thought that she might have said 'come down again' or 'nice to see you', but I should have know better by then. I was still struggling with trying to get some word or praise, anything out of her that resembled love.

I returned home. I hadn't told anyone that I had been to Mother's, I always felt so wrong that I kept returning to the family home after all she had done to me.

I still felt that I wanted to die and the feeling was getting stronger each day. Finally I had to do something about it. I overdosed. I came round as usual in hospital, being questioned as to why I had done it and as usual I couldn't tell them. I didn't know.

Of course I had blown it at my digs. Who wants a suicidal idiot living with them, especially as I couldn't give them a reason for doing it in the first place? It wasn't that I had being unhappy there.

The usual procedure after a suicide attempt was to see a shrink. This time it was a new one, from York. My opinion on meeting him was 'what a stupid old guy'; he said he thought I should go into his mental hospital at York. I wasn't so sure; the last time I was stuck inside one I couldn't get out.

However, it seemed I didn't have any option, I could either go in voluntarily or they could take out an injunction and make me. If I went in on my own accord then at least I could discharge myself any time I wanted.

I asked if someone could contact my mother and let her know where I was, that I was homeless and could I come home when it was OK to leave the hospital. I knew what the answer would be, but at least it was worth a try, I had nowhere else to go.

I thought the hospital was really awful; they all seemed to be spaced out to me, yet here I was. I must have seemed the same to them, too. They came back to me with Mother's answer, 'No'. She didn't want me there as I had always been a problem and she didn't want the kids to see me because she was convinced they would end up following my ways. She persuaded me that she was right, that I was a problem.

So there I was, stuck again in hospital, but this time I knew that I would do my best to get out. I certainly wasn't going to stop in there. I bought the local paper every evening as there were ads for lodgers wanted, but very rarely in my home town. It never entered my head to move areas, and I would have been too afraid to do so in any case. I had been at the hospital about a fortnight when there was an ad in the paper for a lodger wanted in my area. Of course I had to lie when I phoned up about it, I couldn't say that I was at present in a mental hospital as I wouldn't stand a chance of getting it.

I arranged to look at them the next day. I told the hospital that I had somewhere to go and I wanted to discharge myself. They weren't very happy, but this time there was nothing they could do. I never thought about the possibility of not getting the digs: I would cross that bridge when I came to it. The digs were nothing special and the woman was so straight-faced she frightened me slightly, but it was like I had burnt my bridges and felt I had to take them.

The woman's husband had left her several years ago and she had one son. He would be about thirty-five at a guess, but he was backward and had the mind of a ten-year-old. He was quite harmless and just wanted someone to talk to and take a bit of notice of him. We all wanted that, but all people did with him was to take the mickey and he didn't deserve that.

Unfortunately I wasn't there that long. One night I went out with Barry for a drink. As I rarely drank the alcohol soon took affect and I ended up the worse for wear and the more it took affect the more I wanted, it just seemed to make all my problems disappear. Barry had to carry me home, but on the way home I collapsed and he couldn't bring me round so he panicked. He rang for an ambulance and then had to inform my landlady that I would not be returning that evening,

He told her why and her response was that she wasn't having that under her roof, so to speak, and I would have to find somewhere else to go. You would have thought that I made a regular habit of it, but she had spoken and there was no second chance as far as she was concerned.

Blown it again, it seemed I couldn't do anything right. *Mother is right: I am a problem and cause problems wherever I go.* I returned home again on the condition that I finished with Barry. So that's what I did once again. Why he didn't find someone else I never would know. He could have any girl he wanted, they were all better than me, but he never did. He never gave up and he knew me so well that he knew where to find me when I was out. As far as Mother was concerned we had finished, but we still met each other in town and would go out to the cinema, anywhere out of the way so we didn't get found out. I think I was flattered. He made me feel like I was wanted and loved and that wasn't something that I had felt very much. He made me feel good. Yes, he wanted something in return, I suppose, but then between couples it was quite natural to make love, the only purpose it had for me was to create babies. What anyone else saw in it as regards pleasure I will never know to this day. What I wanted was a child of my own and the whole sex act over with as soon as possible. But then I got it fixed in my head that I couldn't have children, something seemed to stick that my mother said something at one time about it.

Things weren't too bad at home. Whatever Mother did to me was made better by the love my younger brother and I shared. He was the special one to me, when I was at home he always came to me for whatever he wanted. Later on in life I found out that it was due to the fact that I would buy him everything he wanted, and not down to loving me. It was down to the fact that I was stupid.

I still bought presents for my mother and treated her, but still never got anything from her in the way of praise or love. Things got worse on the money front as she kept putting up my lodge and as I wasn't on a big wage I couldn't afford it, but no amount of begging or pleading with her would change her mind, it seemed that she just didn't want me to have any money myself. All she would say was that if I didn't like it I could get out. What was the point in moving, as I only seemed to blow that and there were very few places one could go in our town.

So I got another job as well as my daytime one, working in a fish shop in town. The owner had a reputation for being a hard man to get on with, but I got on with him OK. All he asked for was that the job be done correctly and I can say that I couldn't wish for a better boss.

His wife was another matter. She was backward and he had only married her as she was pregnant. Sometimes she would wind you up, but she was really good-hearted and had an awful lot to put up with. Her husband beat her, he had a very short temper as far as his wife and family were concerned and he was a bit of a womaniser. I only interfered once and he told me that it had nothing to do with me and that it didn't affect my work, but I found it very embarrassing. Their private quarters were a part of the fish shop and one couldn't help but hear them.

You would think that I would be used to it as it had been a part of my life for so long at home – it still went on at home – but I never did get used to or understand that kind of thing and I never will.

I worked there four nights a week as well as my day job, so there wasn't much time for anything else really. I saw Barry on the weekends only, but at least it solved the money problem at home with Mother. Perhaps if I hadn't been so daft with my money giving presents all the time I wouldn't have had to work so much, but it gave me more pleasure to give than to receive. In fact still to this day I find it hard to receive things from anyone and I get quite emotional and embarrassed by it. I can never believe that anyone likes me well enough to give me anything or be nice without wanting something back.

There was a new member of staff at the café where I still spent a great deal of my time and we soon became friends even though she was years older than me. She had two sons and one daughter, her youngest son was about fourteen at a guess. She invited me round one day to meet them all and have a cuppa. She must have seen something that I didn't. I think I probably had the word 'sucker' stuck to my forehead.

XI

Barry wanted me to learn to drive as he said then I could drive his car. I wasn't happy about driving his car in case something happened to it, so we went to Darlington and I bought my own car for the great sum of £35. It was a great big thing, an Austin A40 and I didn't think that I could drive it. Barry said of course I could and thinking back he was very good with me as I wasn't the most patient person. I went out with him one day and he said that I was too near the kerb, then that I was too near the middle of the road – I got out of the car and told him to drive the bloody thing himself.

Of course Barry had to take the car back to Middlesbrough with him as I couldn't tell Mother he was teaching me. Maybe when I had a licence she would be OK with him, as I could then take her and the kids out for the day. Barry had a lot of patience with me I must admit, when I lost it he just laughed. I have to laugh myself now thinking about it, as when I used to change gear I would take my hands off the steering wheel and my eyes off the road. It wasn't long before Barry was on about marriage again, well why not get it all booked and sorted out, maybe Mother would change her mind and come after all.

The women from the café said that they would give me all the help I wanted, one of them said that she would do all the catering and that would be her present to us and we could have the do at her house. So we went ahead and booked the registry office. We had two months to prepare. Maybe things would work out all right in the end. I had some daft idea in my head at that time that if we got married then sex wouldn't be too bad, maybe even improve, and that I would get rid of the thoughts and feelings for women that I had. But how wrong can one be?

I still worked like hell during the day and at nights at the fish shop, but didn't mind really because it kept me out of Mother's way and so I couldn't get in trouble with her so much if she didn't see me.

The two months soon went by we had found somewhere to live just outside town in a caravan. It was quiet and cosy, or so I thought, at least it was my own home and I could come and go when I pleased, and eat what I wanted. Selfish really, as Barry never even came onto my thoughts. I was like a little child with a new toy. I would have to tell Mother soon and I wasn't looking forward to that, but I still thought deep down that she would come to the wedding. What a fool I was.

She did her normal thing when I told her, calling me a deceitful bitch and a slut. She said that I would never be happy as Barry was no good and that I could get out of her house because she wanted nothing to do with me. One of the women from the café, in fact the one that hadn't been there very long at all, put me up and it was only a week before the wedding. The week before I got wed I managed to lose my job. It was my fault; I had painted the entire café under the manager's instruction, only to find out that he had put in a bill for it to the owner. I felt so used again. The fact that I hadn't had to paint the place in the first place, but had done so and not been appreciated for it made me say things that I shouldn't. I always opened my mouth without thinking. Anyway, I was dismissed. Good start to married life, but at least I still had the fish shop.

I went to the job centre and luck must have been with me for once as there was a job advertised for a forecourt attendant. I applied for the position and was told to start in a week's time. It was a good job that we weren't going away after the wedding.

Barry planned to go straight back to work on the Monday as he still had his job in Middlesbrough, but he was quite happy to live in my town.

The big day, so to speak, soon came round and I walked down to the registry office with the women from the café. When we arrived Barry's car wasn't there and my first thought was, *Good now I don't have to do it*. I knew that I was making a big mistake when his car drove round the corner and my heart sank. The women didn't pick up anything from me, but then that was me – no one ever knew what my real feelings were about anything. I always keep things back from people, and still do to this day, it's like if I give all of myself then I am open to hurt.

What I should have done there and then was to call it all off, but I couldn't let everyone down after they had gone to so much trouble for me with the reception, and I couldn't hurt Barry. So I came out of there a married woman. Any other woman would have been happy, but not me, and there was now no turning back. We went off to the woman's house that did the catering. She had really put herself out, even made a cake, all I can say is that for her sake I am pleased that I didn't call it off.

All I proceeded to do was get drunk, that way I could blot out what I had just done. Everyone thought that I was just happy and that's what I wanted them to think, I wouldn't let anyone know what was really going through my mind.

Eventually it was all over and we had to go back to the caravan. At least I would have a quiet night as Barry's brother had been the best man and he had to stay over with us till the next day. The next day Barry and I were taking him home and seeing the in-laws.

All I wanted to do when I got in was go to sleep by myself owing to the amount of alcohol that I had drunk. Of course Barry had other ideas and there were the usual jokes off my brother-in-law. I found it all very disturbing and told Barry that we would make up for it the following evening. I would at least have a night to prepare myself. The thing was that I just wasn't interested in sex with any man, but considering it as part of my duty as his wife, at least I would do my best for him. We took his brother back the next day. Barry's mam spent time telling me what he liked to eat and in his pack. I got on very well with them, but it seemed strange to me – remember that I had never learnt to cook, but I guessed that would all have to change. At least it didn't sound too bad; Barry's mam said that he wasn't one for cooked dinners, he preferred chips and snacks. We drove back home, Barry let me drive half way, and then he said that he didn't want me to get too tired. He chatted away; he was a really nice guy and we got on well together, in fact if it wasn't for the sex I could have stopped with him for the rest of my life. He told me that I would make a very good driver one day.

We arrived home about six and decided to get some fish and chips for tea. I suggested that we get a few beers as well, he liked a drink so I knew that would be OK and it would help me cope with what was to come. Perhaps it would have been better if I had told Barry about my father and what went on in my family, but I never did tell him any of that. He just thought that my mother didn't like him and that that was why she threw me out and did the things she did. It would certainly have helped the start of our life together if I hadn't had feelings for a certain woman that I knew. She had just moved as well, so all the time I was thinking of how I could get up to the town where she lived.

Well, I was to start the new job the next day, and was looking forward to it too. I liked dealing with the public, though it was also the fact that they didn't know me and so couldn't criticise me. They just took me as a bit of a fool who liked a laugh and joked with them. There was a young man there called Tom and I had to be trained by him and work with him most of the time. It wasn't too long before he was telling me about his life, I seemed to have that affect on people. They confided in me. It turned out that he was engaged to a young lady that he had grown up with and it was expected by the family that they would get married one day. The problem as far as he was concerned was that he said he didn't have the feelings that he should have for her.

He said that it was OK when he made love to her if he thought that he was with a man or rather pretended that he was with a man. I knew exactly what he was talking about, it seemed that I was not the only one in this world that has feelings for the same sex. I told him to break it off with her and live his life the way he wanted. I never told him about the way I felt, but later on in my life he told me that he knew anyway. That's me: good at giving advice and listening to other people's problems, but no good at talking to anyone about my own.

The boss at the garage was that way inclined as well. He used to lock himself in the toilets with his friend who was a married man. I was really thick, but it was Tom who told me what was going on. Still he was a good boss and even though he knew that I didn't have a driving licence, he would still let me put the cars away at night. Barry and I got on all right until it came to bedtime and I couldn't keep making excuses, and I think I could have put up with the physical side of the whole thing, but it made me sick.

I began wishing I hadn't ruined his life, it was very unfair of me, all I could think about was seeing the woman that I was mad about.

Tom asked the boss if we could have a car to go up to the town where she lived. She didn't know how I felt of course, she just thought that I was a good friend, and that was fine by me as I wouldn't have known what to do about it anyway. It was just nice to see her and be with her. In those days I was very easily satisfied. Barry had my car at that time as his had broken down one night when we had being to see his parents.

It wasn't very long before I had made up another bed in the caravan, I used the excuse that I wasn't used to sleeping with anyone, but I think he knew that there was more to it than that. He came in one pay night and put his pay on the side as he usually did. We went to our separate beds and Barry was in bed asking if he could come over to my bed. Of course I refused and next thing I knew he had jumped out of bed saying that if I wasn't going to be a proper wife then he didn't have to support me. Fair enough, I could handle that, but I did tell him that he would have to pay half the bills. I felt really awful about the whole affair, but knew that I couldn't be a proper wife in that department.

The next day Barry had gone out to work before me so I didn't see him, but noticed he had left his money for me on the side. I decided I would cook him something that he really liked for his supper. I went off to do my shift, which was two till ten that week. That evening I told Barry we hadn't got a future together. I told him that things were all over, but what can I say except that I felt for him. He was very upset, of course. We had only been married two weeks, but I felt a sense of relief after I had spoken to him. He packed some things and drove off into the night. I have to admit, I was happy when he had gone, but I knew I had been a bastard to him.

I felt brave the next day and drove my car to work. There wasn't the amount of traffic on the road then and I figured that I would have to learn myself now that Barry had left me, and I managed quite well really.

I arranged to go to see my friend with Tom that evening as I didn't have to rush home for any reason now, I didn't tell anyone that my husband had left me as I really didn't know how to tell them and I knew it was all my fault that he had gone. Tom and I stopped over for the night at my friend's and I was quite happy with that.

If only I dared do something about the way I felt, but I didn't know how to deal with it. I tried to tell myself that it wasn't normal and it was just a stupid sort of crush. I wish I knew then what I know now, things would have been very different. I went home the next day after my shift only to find that Barry had returned home. He wasn't there, but his pint pot of tea was standing on the side and it hadn't been made long, which meant he couldn't be too far away.

The only way I knew how to deal with it back then was to put his things on the doorstep and lock myself in. What a bitch, what a really rotten piece of work I was. The truth is I was a coward. I had no idea how to face up to things.

He soon turned up asking me to let him in as he wanted to talk to me, he was sure we could work things out. I told him there was nothing to work out that he had left me and he shouldn't have returned. He went away and came back about an hour later with one of the women from the café. I wish he hadn't involved anyone else, but it was too late.

I had to let them in and now there were two of them to deal with. How could I possibly explain to Lilly how I felt about things? I couldn't. She said that I hadn't even given it a fair go and that Barry loved me. I knew all that, but told her that he would be better off with someone else as I couldn't give him everything that he wanted, that I knew I had made a mistake and that I wanted to get out off it. Barry said that he was going to move back in and he would do his best to make it work and wasn't giving up on me. I told him that if he was moving back in then I would be moving out as I couldn't stay. I knew it wouldn't work and I didn't want to try.

I just left them there; I walked out, got into my car, drove to the lay-by and spent the night in the car. I was on duty the next day at 6 a.m. I finished my shift at 2 p.m., then spent the rest of the day in the café and in the car. I figured out that I could stay in the garage during my time off as I had keys to open up, at least it would give me a bit of breathing space until I could come up with something better.

A lot of the evenings I went up to my friend's and stayed there, which was perfect. All I wanted was to be with her.

I got away with staying at the garage for about a fortnight and then the boss found out. He was very good about it really and said that I could go home with him that weekend. I could give his house a good clean as repayment, but I would have to sort something out as regards accommodation.

Eventually, I had to return home. I couldn't keep crashing with other people, and you can imagine the stick and the humble pie I had to eat at home as regards my mother's 'I told you so' attitude, but she was right I shouldn't have got married. Mind you, if she had been OK with me all these years then I wouldn't have wanted to get away in the first place. Of course I couldn't have said that to her, I just had to tell her she was right in everything she said and that I would listen to her in future. About the only thing that pleased her was the fact that I had a car. It didn't bother her that I wasn't legal, though no doubt if I got caught she would have said 'I told you so' and deny that she ever knew anything about it.

Well at least I had Tom to have a laugh with at work and go out with. He and I got on really well and some of the things we did we would have got into trouble with the boss for. We would take the car out at night without permission and go up to Middlesbrough and have a night out and a few laughs. Tom would always drive so at least if we got stopped we were legal. Other times we would turn the lights off early on the forecourt when a customer had pulled in for petrol and hide under the desk watching them. It doesn't seem funny now, but then we thought it was very funny.

Well, here I was, nearly twenty-three years old, and what had I got – still living with Mother and no money because I always spent it on my mother and brothers and sister. I was still trying to buy their love; I knew by that point that it didn't work, but I never learnt.

It wasn't long before Mother threw me out again. I can't even remember why, but then she didn't really need a reason. She was the boss and I was just a piece of dirt under her feet. Was there any wonder that I thought nobody liked me and that I was never good enough for anyone?

I went to live at the Black Bull pub on a bed and breakfast agreement so found it a bit hard with the money as I had to buy the rest of my meals.

I put in for my driving test and on the morning I had to take it my car broke down – the story of my life it seemed. The boss at the garage said that I could take the little Hornet on my test, but what he failed to tell me was that the handbrake wasn't working properly, but then it was good of him to lend me it in the first place. Needless to say I failed my test. Mother would have crowed if she had known.

There was two boys living at the pub at that time as well and I got on well with them. We used to take the landlady's car, with her permission, leave early in the morning and go trout fishing. It was interesting, I never knew what anyone saw in fishing until then.

Soon after that Tom and I found out that the garage was closing and we would soon be out of a job. Since we had met and got to know each other he had fallen in love with a local boy and they were talking about moving in together. Good for him, at least he had the guts to do what he wanted to do with his life. He took a bit of stick from the people in the town, but his parents stood by him and gave him all the support he needed.

So it was time to find another job and move on. I applied to a new chicken factory that had just opened about twelve miles away. the only problem was that of transportation, but the landlady said I could borrow her car until I got sorted out. I didn't like deceiving her as she thought that I had a licence, but I didn't have much choice really. I got the job owing to the fact that I had done it before and they tested me out there and then on the trussing section. I never liked starting a new job as I didn't like getting to know new people, but before I knew where I was, I was soon a part of factory life again, among the jokes, teasing and crudeness that went with it. You either went with it or you were a misfit and treated as such.

I worked with a girl called Norah. She lived in the town where the factory was and even though I thought she was young, she already had eight children. She went on to have eleven children altogether, but I must admit she was a fair, but strict mother and all her children knew their place. I say this as I went to her house several times and eventually moved in as a lodger when my landlady decided to leave the pub, which left me without transport to get to work. Norah and I got on well and as for the children, I was used to kids. Her husband was a bit of a ladies' man, and crude with it, but he thought he was funny with some of the things he came out with as regards their sex life. I was certainly surprised at the fact that Norah wasn't embarrassed about the things he said and found it a bit much at first, but soon got used to his ways.

There were two men in the factory, one fancied Norah and the other one fancied me. I was flattered as usual and seeing as I didn't want anyone to know or guess that I felt things for women I decided to give it a try with this man. We started going out together, he was a real mammy's boy and very quiet, but he was nice with me. Norah started seeing the other man on the side. It turned out that she wasn't very happy in her marriage and it wasn't long before she and her husband parted. Later she married this man and they are still together to this day.

My new man took me to meet his mother. She certainly wasn't pleased that her son had brought someone home to meet her as he didn't usually do things like that. She thought it was serious and was frightened I was going to take her little boy away, if only she knew that there was no chance of that.

All I ever wanted out of any man was my own child, but I thought that would never happen. I had been at the factory about a year when I got called into the personnel department. It turned out that someone had put in a complaint that I was a lesbian and that I had made advances towards them. I resented that as I had never done anything wrong apart from the fact that I wouldn't admit to myself that I was one and didn't know how to make advances. I told personnel that I had a boyfriend and whoever had said that was talking a load of rubbish. She said that it had been two people that had complained and she suggested that I keep away from said people as, if there was another complaint, she would have to sack me. It wouldn't happen these days, but I was very easily intimidated then. It has only in my later years that I have started to defend myself.

I actually saved some money while staying at Norah's as I didn't see much of the family then, only went through about once every month. They never really missed me as much as I missed them anyway.

My new man wanted to get more serious, he asked me to marry him. I didn't tell him that I had been married and I didn't want to go there again. *Why can't men just enjoy the company of a woman without taking it one step further?* Yes, I ended up having a sexual relationship with him, if that's what you can call it, but all I wanted out of it was a child and anyone would do. The relationship didn't last too long after that as I started going out with a girl from work. It was nothing serious, more experimental than anything else. I took her to my home town as that was familiar ground and I didn't want anyone talking at the factory. We went for a few drinks and it was in the back room of the pub. We were the only ones there so it was easy to kiss her without anyone seeing. She wouldn't let me touch her so I guess I really took advantage of her as she was rather the worse for wear, but I had to know how it felt to get close to a woman. I wish that I could say that I fancied her, but I didn't really. However, I got turned on kissing her. It felt good and very different to what it felt like with a man. If only I could face up to what I was, but I kept denying everything.

It was a big mistake taking this girl out, she thought I wanted her and started avoiding me. In fact, judging by the whispers and strange looks, she must have told some people in the factory. It wasn't long before I was taken up to the office again, only this time I was informed that I had been fired owing to the complaints about my sexual advances. This made me even more determined to never let anyone know what I was thinking or feeling. That way no one could get anything on me or hurt me in any way. As soon as someone got close to me I would put up a wall as a barrier and each time I felt that a brick was coming down off my wall then I would start lying, not serious lies, but just enough to fool the person that was getting close to me so that no one ever really got to know the real me.

XII

As there were no jobs in the area, after losing the factory one I moved back to my old town and back home to my family. Of course Mother was rather pleased as she would have an extra income so the heat was on to find a job and quickly as I couldn't stand being at home all day.

My sister now had my old room and she was ten years old, it was fun really sharing it with her. I didn't used to like getting ready for bed when she was there and she found that strange, but that was another thing about me, I didn't like anyone seeing my body. She used to laugh at me when I jumped into bed because I had to go through my ritual of looking under the bed before I turned off the light and then pulling the covers over my head.

I remember one night in particular, I came in after going to the café and went to bed as normal, but had got it in my head that someone was coming to get me with a knife. My sister laughed, but I could even hear someone coming up the stairs. I think my sister realised that I was really scared when I started to shake and cry. She was really good, she got out of bed and turned on the light, we cuddled up together and I eventually fell to sleep. I have had this terrible feeling since then and it was very real to me.

I soon got a job at the local egg packers. It was a bit like a factory job, but not on such a large scale; there were only about twelve women there and possibly six drivers, but we very rarely saw them. There was one woman there named was Julie, and boy did I fancy her, but she certainly wasn't gay. She had a husband and he was in the army, we became friends and I met her husband. She occasionally came out in the car with me and when her husband went away with the army, she asked me to stay at her house as she didn't like to be by herself.

I did make a pass at her one night, and we would kiss and touch when her husband was away, but I felt guilty about this and eventually had to tell her husband what I had done.

He was very understanding, but I didn't spend any more time there and it wasn't long before she left the area. I did hear through the grapevine that they stayed together and went on to have a family. I was pleased that I didn't split them up, I don't think I could have coped with that, but I vowed never to get into that situation again. That was easier said than done, as I found out in later life.

Things weren't too bad at home apart from money, which Mother seemed to be obsessed with. I remember hiding a ten shilling note once in my jacket pocket in the wardrobe where I thought no one would look, but Mother found it. My big brother seemed to take all that he wanted; if he liked something then he took it. There was no point in saying anything as nothing was ever done about it and I would only be accused of trying to cause trouble.

The factory job was going OK, nothing ever came out of what happened with Julie, and my old job was up for grabs again at the fish shop, so I got that back. I know it didn't leave me any time for myself, but that's really the way I liked it. I thought that way there would be no chance of me getting into any affairs or any bother.

The boss at the fish shop used to take his holidays and leave the place for me to run, the fact that anyone trusted me alone with their business made me feel good. There were two girls working there, one I had gone to school with and the other one a couple years younger. She had been in trouble with the law and the boss was the only one who gave her a chance by employing her. We all got on very well and the place ran like clockwork while he was away.

It wasn't long before Mother was on her usual path of wanting more lodge money. My big brother never had this problem, but then I figured out that she was probably as frightened of him as she was my father. He seemed to have the same temper as Father. I suppose she found it hard with all the kids to bring up and as they wouldn't part with any of their money, it was down to me. The only trouble was that I didn't have an endless supply. The car was an expense, but I loved driving and enjoyed taking Mother and the kids out on the weekend. She was slightly different when she got away from the house and Father, in fact sometimes we had a laugh together.

Even though my brothers and sister were growing up it still gave me great pleasure to treat them. My little brother was still the one that got everything off me and he used to know that I was a soft touch. He was now at school, the second-born in the new family. He was different somehow, a bit of a clown and sad-looking really. The other one was the brains in the family, he had passed his 11+, and he certainly was Mother's little boy. He was my grandfather's favourite as well, in fact when he had to study for exams he would go up to my grandparents so he could have the peace and quiet that he needed.

It wasn't long before Mother threw me out again. It seemed that she couldn't put up with me for too long and had to have a go, the only way she could get to me these days was to throw me out on the street.

I would go out in the car and when I came back the door would be locked and she would tell me that I had to find some-where else to live, no explanation. Sometimes she would have my clothes on the step and sometimes I had to start all over again buying clothes. It was slightly annoying walking up the street and seeing a girl with the things on her back that I had bought and my mother had gone and sold them.

Sometimes I would be lucky and find lodgings pretty quickly, other times I had to sleep in barns and have to get washed in the public toilets. I got to be an old hand at it after a while and no one even knew what was going on or where I was living.

I found digs about a mile out of town. They weren't bad people, just a bit set in their ways, so to speak, very routine. The only problem was that I never had a key and so had to be in at set times, but through them I met Peggy. She was a woman that my landlady worked with and on the odd occasions when they didn't have a lift to work of an evening I used to take them. Peggy was on her second marriage and had five children at that time and she certainly knew how to enjoy herself. Her husband was really soft with her and she did basically what she wanted to do, which included going out with other guys. I spent quite a bit of time at her house and she kept asking me to move in. I would have loved to, but I felt that I was not being fair to my landlady if I did so has she was the one who had introduced us in the first place.

As it turned out things were taken out of my hands, so to speak. I needed to get in my digs one day and having no key climbed in through the window. I got washed and changed and went out again. I guess I shouldn't have done that, but as usual for me I never even thought about it, I just did it. My landlady wasn't happy about it at all – she couldn't see why I couldn't have waited for her to return home. Peggy said that I should have had a key in the first place and for a short while they fell out over the issue. But it ended up with me going to live at Peggy's.

I shared a room with her young daughter who was ten years old at that time. Her youngest was about four and a half, it reminded me of home and my family. I had moved jobs by this time and now worked on a turkey farm, which I enjoyed. The money was very good and I used to travel all over the countryside.

It was a dirty job, but then that didn't worry me, as soon as I got home I would have a bath and get changed. That was some-thing new to me also because at home one wasn't allowed to bathe whenever you wanted.

Of a weekend, Peggy would go down to a big dance place about twenty-seven miles away. She kept on at me to go, but I never had the confidence to go somewhere like that, I would always feel like a fish out of water. On the evenings when she had finished work we would sit in her other room, as she called it, and have a few drinks and just talk. She told me that she had the hots for a guy at work and she had been out with him once or twice, she also had a bit of a thing for the club collector who came to the house every week. I actually talked to her about my feelings for women, but all she ever said about that was all I needed was a good man and the rest was all in my head. I wished I could believe that, but I knew what I felt.

She had a brother as well, he would call in at odd times, and had seemed to be calling in quite a lot. Peggy ended up telling me that he wanted to take me out, but was too shy to ask. She seemed to think that it was great and kept on about how she would like me for a sister-in-law. I must admit that she would be a wonder-ful sister-in-law and I had met all the family including her parents. I wondered if I could make a go of it with him, he seemed nice enough. I was still trying to pretend that I was 'normal'. I remember seeing the shrink on one occasion and he told me that I was a lesbian. I walked home that day telling myself that I wasn't. The worst thing is admitting it to oneself, after that the rest seems to come quite easily.

So there I was, still trying to fool everyone, including myself, that I was OK and had boyfriends, which is precisely why I started going out with Peggy's brother.

He had been married, I found out, and had two children from that union. My mind was working overtime here, remember that it was all I had ever wanted to have my own child. Selfish I suppose really, when you think that I would be using him, but I didn't think like that I'm afraid. I didn't know the real reason then as to why he and his wife split up and I guess that I didn't really care that much either. Peggy persuaded us to go dancing with her one evening and, like I said, it wasn't really me. I had never had the chance to learn how to dance but didn't want to tell them why I didn't dance, just said that I didn't want to and left it at that.

One day I came in from work to find that my mother had been up to see Peggy. I thought that after she had put her oar in Peggy wouldn't want anything to do with me.

I was wrong. Peggy said that Mother had told her how I was violent, kept overdosing and that I stole – you name it and according to my mother I did it – but Peggy hadn't taken a blind bit of notice. She had told my mother that as far as she was concerned I had never done her any harm and she thought I was a nice person and she took people how she found them.

I guess Mother had heard through the grapevine that I was happy living there and so she thought that she would put a stop to my being happy, but for once it didn't work.

Peggy was now seeing a soldier and things weren't that good between her and her husband. In fact, it came out that her husband had been getting off with her eldest son's girlfriend who was living with us at the time as Peggy's son had joined the army and he was down south. Peggy threw her husband out and told the girl that she would have to return home and she would go down and explain to her son what had happened. So we drove all the way down and reached there in the early hours of the morning. I didn't mind as I liked driving and wanted to help her with the problem. As it was too early to knock anyone out of bed, we went to a lay-by to try and get a bit of sleep as it was going to be a long day. We ended up getting pulled in by the police and had to explain why we were kipping in a lay-by. They were very good and took us back to the station where Peggy managed to get a cup of tea out of them – you have to admire her nerve, because although we had done nothing wrong I was terrified.

Her elder son was upset of course, but there wasn't a lot he could do about it, short of going absent without leave, which he didn't want to do, thank God. It was a bit of a bad journey home as the car pulled to one side. On looking at it I found the chassis leg had come all the way through the boot, but just told Peggy that it was nothing and prayed that it would get us home OK.

In the meantime her brother and I had started a relationship. I wish that I could say that it was satisfactory, but I started noticing things about him, like how he was with his money – let's call it tight – and there were other things about him that reminded me of my father. Since Peggy and her husband had parted she had filled in a form to have a council house as she could no longer keep the mortgage payments up and her husband wouldn't support the kids or anything. He said that it was all her fault that he had gone with someone else and she was a slut.

I, on the other hand, wasn't feeling too good and Peggy sent me to the doctor's. Well, it had taken a long time and I never thought that it was possible, but I was pregnant. I phoned up for the results and the doctor said he wanted to see me. My mind worked overtime, what if something was wrong? I didn't know that I had to get booked into a hospital and things like that, I just thought the worst. When I saw the doctor and he said about it being a bit old to be having my first baby, I jumped down his throat and said that I wasn't getting rid of it. I knew that he was only talking to me really, but it still made me mad.

Of course Peggy was over the moon and so was her brother. Now the problem was how to tell my mother. Peggy said she had a right to know that she was going to be a grandmother and that maybe she would be happy for me for once. The best thing to do, Peggy said, was to write her a letter, as I didn't feel brave enough to talk to her at all. Rather silly when you think that I was nearly twenty-seven years old and still scared of what my mother thought or what she could do. I did know one thing though, there was no way anyone would take this baby off me.

I went down on one of the days Mother went to my grandparents to clean the house – my grandmother wasn't well at that time, and very shortly after she died. She never knew about her great grandchild, but then seeing as I wasn't married it was maybe as well, as she had very old fashioned ideas. It was a miscalculation on my behalf I'm afraid, but when I got to the house I could see someone inside so I pushed the letter through the letterbox and ran like hell. I had no sooner got back to Peggy's and the phone rang. It seemed Mother was over the moon, or so Peggy said. I didn't have the guts to talk to her right then, but she said that she didn't realise that I had been seeing anyone, as if she took an interest in me anyway.

Peggy's brother decided we should go down and see her, after all, he didn't know her, in fact no one knew her really except me, she could fool anyone into thinking what a nice woman she was and how I couldn't be right with some of the things that I said about her. She was her charming self when we went down, how happy she was that I had found someone to settle down with and had we plans to get married, where were we going to live, all the nice questions. If only they knew. No doubt I would get all the hassle at a later date. Anyway I didn't really care all that much as I had what I had wanted for years – my own child on the way. I knew that it would never want for anything and that it would never feel unloved or not wanted and no one would ever take this baby off me, it wasn't like a dog, it couldn't be gassed.

My father was in hospital at that time having a hip replacement. Well, after he had it Mother wanted me to take her to see him. I felt almost sorry for him laid there, but after a few minutes that soon changed. His temper hadn't improved while he was there and he embarrassed my mother with his foul language, but that didn't bother him. Mother told him he was going to be a granddad, but there was no reaction really. But I knew that I would make sure that, if it was a girl, he would have nothing to do with it that's for sure.

I started getting things ready for my baby; even though it was very early days, it was going to have everything. Around about this time I started to find out what kind of a father Peggy's brother would make. It seemed that his drink was more important to him than parting with any money for his child. He reminded me of my father at that time, and even though I had thought about stopping with him for the sake of my child I was certainly having second thoughts now. His other sister who lived away from the town where we lived said that one of the reasons his wife had left him was because of his drinking and the fact that he didn't want to part with any money for his family. She said to order some things on his account out of her catalogue and then he would have to pay for them. I didn't think that was a good idea, as to me it was deceitful, but we agreed to get two dozen nappies and tell her brother when I got home.

His reaction wasn't a good one. He said that I had no right to do such a thing and his sister shouldn't have let me order anything. It seemed that he thought he had me trapped now that I was pregnant, well he could think again. I got no invites to go out with him any more and he had the old-fashioned idea that women should stop at home when they were in that condition, so off he would go to the pub. I tried talking to Peggy about the situation, but she just seemed to think that he was worried about me and wanted me to stay at home and rest as I was still working. She said he just worried about things. I suppose he was her brother and at the end of the day she would defend him against anyone else; I would defend my family also.

The final thing that made my mind up happened when he came in from the pub on evening. He was in a foul mood and because I answered him back I got a smack round the head and was thrown on the bed. That was my father all over. I decided there and then that it wasn't the life I wanted for my child; I didn't want it to grow up among violence like I had. I would wait until tomorrow and pack my things and go home once again. Mother gave me a real lecture about my child growing up without a father and she had thought that I was going to settle down with this man, he seemed like a nice chap and what was my problem. I couldn't tell her that my child would be better off with only one parent that really loved it than with two parents that fought all the time and violence and fear. She would have just said that it hadn't done me any harm and that I should be thankful that any man, or anyone wanted to take me on.

The next thing that happened was the loss of my job at the egg packers. It certainly didn't come at a good time as I was nearly five months pregnant and no one would want to employ a pregnant woman. I applied for a job cleaning out turkey sheds and didn't tell them I was expecting as I needed the job to provide for my child. The work was very manual and all I wanted to do when I came home was to sleep, I suffered with sickness all day long and had to spend my days trying to hide it from my employers.

My young sister was very excited about the baby and used to joke about my big tummy in bed of a night; my brothers, if not the eldest, were so looking forward to being uncles, especially the second-born one, the sad-looking one. He was so funny, but then he was so different to the rest of us. He always used to come to me when he was upset and I would listen to him and give him a smoke. I always wanted to love him, but he shied away from that.

He came in one day and stuck his head round the door, he had been for a hair cut, but he had a Mohican! Just a tuft of hair running down the middle of his head and a stupid grin on his face. Mother went spare and said that he would have to face up to it at school, but he didn't care about that very much as he never liked school anyway. It was like the time he came in and tried to do his kung fu bit and ended up falling flat on his face, but he only laid there laughing – that was my brother for you.

Getting back to me, it wasn't long before the people at work found out I was expecting, but the boss, being a woman, seemed very understanding and said that, providing I didn't come back on them if anything went wrong, it was OK for me to stay there as long as I could manage.

I bought a pram, a cot and other things for my baby. I bought all the things for a boy not like most people that bought yellows and whites. Perhaps I had fixed it in my head that it had to be a boy because I didn't want a girl where my father was. My aunties, or rather my mother's aunties, knitted things for the baby. Mother didn't knit anything for it, yet later on when my sister had children. She couldn't knit enough for her or do enough for her children, but I was too happy to even realise that at the time.

To make extra money I kept the fish shop job till the last minute. The boss there was very good with me and wouldn't let me do anything that he thought would put either myself or the baby at risk, if only have he could seen what my day job entailed he would have had a fit.

I drove a tractor to pull shavings in the sheds, racked them in and lifted and carried all day long. There were two chaps at that job that were really nice. One was called Henry and the other Gerald. The latter one married a friend of mine in later life and didn't have a very good life towards the end, a real shame as he was a lovely man.

I started mild labour pains on the Thursday and Mother didn't tell me anything so I ended up going to the doctor's. I felt a bit of a fool when he said that the baby would soon be here, Mother could have told me that. Still, she couldn't break the habit of a lifetime and actually give me some support. I told her that I didn't want to go into hospital until the last minute. I went on until the early hours of Sunday morning and by that time Mother was certainly worried and said that she thought something must be wrong and I should go into the hospital, she even had to panic me at the last minute as regards the birth of my baby.

My son was born at lunchtime. It was a difficult birth, but seeing him made everything worthwhile. He was beautiful, with dark black hair and dark brown eyes. He was perfect in every way and all that you could wish for.

His father came to see us the first evening, he had brought a white anorak to fit a one-year-old as it was going cheap in the sales. He had to think of his money. It was at times like that that I was pleased I found out what he was like before it was too late. My son would never feel the loss of a father as I had enough love to give him for two parents.

Mother and Father came in the afternoon to see us both and she actually said that he was a beautiful baby. I didn't really care what she thought of him, but I did know that she would never take him off me or hurt him in any way whatsoever, in fact no one would ever hurt him I would make bloody sure of that.

XIII

So most of my life at that period was spent working and looking after my son, and I must say that he was the best thing that ever happened to me. My other brother had become a chef, or rather was training to become a chef, he was Mother's little pet and she gave him everything that he wanted. Father had lent him the money to buy a car and I taught him to drive, he was a quick learner and passed his test within three months. He never paid Father back any of the money for the purchase of the car. Father kept on at Mother about it, although she wasn't in position to pay him, but did in later years when my grandfather passed away.

To show just how spoilt he was by Mother, well, spoilt full stop really: it wasn't very long before he smashed the car up. He stormed into his room and wrecked it, refusing to come out until they promised to pay for the repair of his car, which of course they did. It wasn't very long before he wrote the car off all together then my father bought a big Volvo and said that it was his car and my brother could use it providing that he was always there to take my father wherever he wanted to go. This arrangement was agreed upon and my brother used it for work every day.

However, one Friday he never came home. My father was furious. He didn't return the next day either. Naturally Mother got all the grief for that. When he did return, he told Mother that he had been to Wales with another guy; he admitted that he was gay and this was one of his flings. All Mother said at that time was, 'you had better tell your father when he comes home.' So when Father came home, my brother stood in front of him and announced that he was gay. My father said that he always knew that there was something wrong with him and he could get out of his house. Then it started with my parents, it was as if they were trying to blame each other for the way my bother was. *Why can't they just except that it wasn't anyone's fault?*

All that episode did was teach me not to say anything about

my feelings, not that there was much chance of that anyway.

My brother moved out the next day, he went into a bedsit about a mile out of town. He must have had it all lined up because places weren't that easy to find. It took my mother about a week and then she asked me to take her down to see him. He had it lovely and seemed quite settled. Of course Mother took him things down for the place, it was all forgiven as far as she was concerned, but she never told anyone all the way through life about her son. She would say that he lived with friends wherever he happened to be at the time, but she never told anyone that he was gay, just that he was too busy with his job or whatever to get married.

Much later he got a crush on a boy that lived in the flat upstairs from him. To cut a long story short, the boy took him for all he could get, and my brother eventually cracking up over it. He spent a lot of time in the local mental hospital. Strangely, he ended up meeting someone in there and never came back to our town at all. He seemed very happy with his new life. At least he had the courage to leave the area, not like me.

As for me well I was expected to drive the car with them everywhere they wanted to go even though I still had my own car at that time. Things were up and down at home, Father was always in a mood over something, usually because he couldn't get the grass cut down at the churchyard in the time that he wanted it done. He had taken over the churchyard about a year before, just after my brother had died. He had felt guilty as he knew that if it hadn't been for him, his son would still be here.

The same day that my son, Christopher, was born, my fifteen-year-old brother Bert had been playing with a football while our parents came to visit me in hospital. It was his prize possession. When they returned home, my sister, Dari, told my parents that Bert had been kicking the ball round the front lawn, which was out of bounds and supposed to be a showpiece for the neighbours. My father was furious. As Bert walked up the path, my father stood in the window and held up the football. He picked up a knife and deliberately slit it top to bottom, destroying it completely.

Bert was distraught. In a moment of retaliation, Bert ran into the shed at the bottom of the garden, attached a rope to a beam and hanged himself. It was Mother who found him, but Father never seemed to get over it.

It was getting me down at home, particularly as there seemed to be a competition between Mother and me as regards my son's affections. He was my son! As far as I was concerned she wouldn't have any say over him. I went to the council and asked them how far I was to getting somewhere to live. I didn't care where as long as I got away from here. They informed me that it would be a while before I got anywhere and I told them if they didn't get me somewhere soon that I would crack up with the situation at home.

Much to my surprise, about a fortnight later they offered me a maisonette with two bedrooms at the other end of the town. It was great! I accepted it immediately. Mother wasn't very pleased, but I didn't care. She said that I couldn't raise my son as I was incapable of looking after myself, let alone a child. I vowed that I would show her different.

I went to the social services to see if I could get any help with furniture and they informed me that because I wasn't on benefits they couldn't help me, so I got rid of my car to buy carpets and a bed and a few things. My boss at the fish shop gave me a table and chairs and I was able to buy a cheap cooker. I soon had a few bits and we moved in. It was a bit of a struggle at first, learning to cook and running a home; I had no washer so I had to boil all my son's things in a pot on the cooker, but the pleasure I got putting all the white nappies out on the line and dressing him was immense. My sister would come up some evenings and look after him; of course, I had to pay her. No one in my family did anything for nothing.

Christopher was now a year and a half old and such a good child, he played in the back garden with his toys and let me get on with things then I used to go and play with him. Fun days, but lonely nights; I wasn't used to being by myself.

I stayed there for two years and then someone wanted an exchange with a place near my parents as they were looking to live in something smaller. As my mother pointed out, she could look after Christopher when I went to the fields to work and I wouldn't be fetching him out early each a morning for her to look after, so it made sense to move. She still controlled my life even then. To a certain extent she did till her death.

So I moved into a three-bedroom house round the corner from my parents. I worked like crazy to build a nice home up for my son and made sure every day that I spent time with him, letting him know how much he meant to me, loving and cuddling him and reading bedtime stories; all the things I never got I made sure he had.

My sister had grown up and started to work with me at the fish shop. We got quite close at that time and she used to ask me to go out with her, which I did occasionally. It wasn't easy getting a babysitter, though, as I refused to just have anyone. Mother found out one night that we had gone out and all hell broke loose. My sister couldn't cope and moved in with me for a short period, short because I couldn't put up with her for long.

Anyway it soon came round to another Christmas and my boss, his wife and the girl that I worked with at the fish shop came down to my place for drinks. Jane, the other girl who I worked with, asked if she could fetch her husband as well, so there were five of us altogether. They all had a drop too much to drink and Jane wasn't feeling too well and ended up in the bathroom throwing up. Her husband didn't seem too bothered, but asked me if I could go and see if she was all right.

I went into the bathroom to find her and she didn't seem too bad. As I made to leave, she grabbed hold of me and started kissing me. It got a bit heavy, I didn't want to stop her, but I had to. Her husband was just in the other room, it wasn't right. We rejoined the others, but by the time she had had another drink she had become really unsteady; her husband asked if I could just put her to bed for a while. Once we were in the bedroom she started kissing me again and trying to pull me into bed with her. It was very hard not to, I found her attractive, but I had sworn never to get involved with a married woman again.

A few hours later her husband got her up and they all went home, thank God. I wouldn't have anyone round again as I felt so bad about what had, or could have, happened.

I saw Jane the next day; her husband wasn't there so it was just the two of us. She said that she hadn't meant to come on to me, but I felt that it was too late. My feelings were already messed up.

I found it very hard working with her after that and started drinking at work to get me through the nights that she was there. Soon my boss realised that something wasn't quite right and he had a talk to me. He had figured out how I felt about Jane and said that he would get rid of her if I found it easier, he didn't want to lose me and he suspected she was stealing from the till anyway. I didn't want to be responsible for her losing her job so I took some leave to get away. I needn't have: as it turns out the decision was soon taken out of our hands as Jane got arrested for the theft of cheque books from a nightclub. She told the newspapers that she was confused as her boss and the girl she worked with were both making advances and she didn't know what she was doing half the time. Clever ploy – everyone in the town knew where she worked. Although nothing was ever said I knew that people were talking.

A year after that they decided to move us out of our houses while they were being modernised and my son and I were placed in another house, this time just five houses away from Mother. Once again she said that it would be easier for me if my son was nearer to her so she could babysit and she was sure if I saw the council that they would leave me there rather than going through the hassle of returning to my old home, once again I listened to her. Now she could really keep her eye on me, but I didn't think of that at the time. She just had to look over and if my curtains were still drawn then it would be 'What time do you call that to get up?' and 'I saw you go out last night!' or whatever she thought she had seen. I knew my life had nothing to do with her, really, but as usual she got to me.

My son was soon to start school and so I needed a job to fit in with his school hours so I bought a set of ladders and started up a window-cleaning round. It was hard work, but at least I could work the hours I wanted and be there to meet Christopher from school at lunchtime and in the evenings. My days seemed to be taken up going backwards and forwards to the school, as he had to come home for lunch until he had attended school for a year.

I still got depressed, but as soon as I felt that I was going down that road I would go back on the antidepressants. The nights were the worst. After my son had gone to bed, I would walk up to the top of the path and stand at the gate hoping someone would walk by, if only to say hello. It helped me to stop feeling so isolated. I never really had any friends as such, just workmates and, of course, my family. I didn't see much of them except for when they wanted something, like babysitting money or for me to drive them somewhere in the car. They wouldn't let me have a car for my own use at all, just to transport them.

Another Christmas approaching, and my son had now reached the age of six and a half – where does time go! I had all his presents wrapped and put away; I loved Christmas with him, he was so pleased with whatever he got, but I always went a bit overboard because I didn't want him to feel left out through not having a father. His father never so much as sent him a card, let alone bought him anything. Still, I didn't care and I don't think Christopher missed not having a father. We always went over to the family home for lunch and I suppose things weren't too bad now, Father only lost his temper these days, but he could still upset my mother by some of the things he said to her.

On Boxing Day they wanted me to take them to the sales at Stockton. We got there and Father stood in front of a washer. I couldn't work out why because Mother had just bought one that year, but he asked me if I would like one. Of course I did and told him that I could never afford one as there was too much else to do in the house. He said that if I wanted it then I could borrow the money and pay back whatever I could afford to each week. Well, I took him up on his offer even though I couldn't work out why he was doing it. I don't know what I was thinking, but he must have known that I wouldn't put up with anything. Maybe it was just guilt for all he had done to me. Anyway, I borrowed money from him for a new freezer and cooker as well as the washer – not all at once, of course.

I had been busy decorating the house all the way through and had noticed this girl who used to walk by on her way to work and back. I knew that she was a lesbian, I heard the kids calling her names. She seemed very quiet and shy and I never saw her with anyone. I wondered what it would be like to really be with a woman. Still, I supposed, I could dream, because she wouldn't want to know me like that I was pretty sure.

One day she passed by at lunchtime and looked up at me in the bedroom window and smiled. She had the most beautiful smile, why it lit up her face. She asked me how the painting was getting on. I said that I had so much to do at the moment. She said she had to go for lunch and she would see me on the way back to work. So I watched for her coming past the house again and this time we talked. She introduced herself as Dee and said that she enjoyed painting and if I wanted a hand she would come and help me on an evening. Of course I jumped at the chance. I couldn't believe she wanted to come into my home to spend any time with me, but she obviously did.

So we arranged for her to come round after she had eaten that evening and got herself sorted out. I couldn't wait to see her and really talk to her, I didn't know what else, but decided I would play it by ear.

Christopher had his bath and I read him his story, but even after he had settled for the night, she still hadn't arrived. I felt deflated; I should have known it was too good to be true. It was nearly eight and there was a very quiet knock on the door; in fact, I wouldn't have heard it if it hadn't been for the little dog that I had purchased for my son about six months before.

Dee came in, in the same things that she had on earlier, but I didn't care what she had on. I made her a drink and said that I didn't feel like painting that evening as I had done enough of it that day and that I hoped she didn't mind if we just sat and talked and played some music or watched the box or whatever she wanted to do.

She seemed OK with that, but she wasn't a great talker, still it was nice to be sat with her. We didn't need to say a lot, and couldn't talk gay issues as Dee was rather embarrassed about what she was, though I didn't find that out till much later. We arranged that she would come round the next night to help with the painting. It was in the early hours that she left that morning; she crept out, looking all around as she left. That was the pattern of things for the next fortnight. We spent every night together. We kissed and that was very heavy, but despite wanting to take it further, we never really did. Once it got too heavy, we would make a drink and settle down again. But I had never felt like this before, I couldn't wait to see her, to be with her and kiss her. Just to feel her body close to mine was enough to make me feel things that I had never known before.

One evening Dee came round and told me that she had taken her driving test that day; I felt disappointed that she hadn't told me the previous evening, but that was how she was and I loved her nonetheless. However, that evening was when I started seeing the other side of her. Dee was rather moody because she had failed her test. I told her that I would teach her to drive as my brother had learnt with me and I would soon be teaching my sister.

She didn't want anyone to know we were even seeing each other. Whenever she came over she would she drew the curtains, and she always left in the early hours of the morning, looking all the time to see if there was anyone around. I couldn't live like that and told her so. I suppose that was our first disagreement. Dee said that perhaps it would be better if we didn't see each other again as she felt it was getting too serious. I begged her not to be like that, I was sure we could work something out, but no, she walked out of the door and said she would see me about.

I didn't quite know what to do because she lodged just round the corner with friends and I knew I would have to see her going to work and returning every day and I couldn't deal with it at all. I had never felt this strongly about anyone before and it was completely new to me, I just knew that I didn't want to be without her. However, I wouldn't beg anyone to see me if they didn't want to.

It hurt me to see her walking by at lunchtime and in the evenings, but I would make sure she didn't see me watching. She always looked at the windows as she went by.

Last thing at night, I would let the dog out. He would run over to the lamppost and start whining, and so I would know that she was standing there. But until she was ready to face up to the fact that we were together and stop sneaking about, there was nothing I felt that I could do. It wasn't that I was asking for a lifetime commitment, just that we could be openly together and go out together just for a walk even.

What made matters worse at that time was the fact that my son had just started having night terrors and they were scary. He would wake up screaming, convinced there was someone behind the curtains with a knife; he would push me away when I went to cuddle him and try to make it all better for him. When he was awake he wouldn't leave me and if I walked up the path on a night he would come running out in his pyjamas after me, so he needed a lot of care and attention at that time. I found out later that these night terrors were being triggered by one of the television programmes he liked and so I had to stop him watching them.

The stand-off with Dee lasted about a week. One night she knocked on the door asking if could she come in and talk to me about things. We just fell into each other's arms and kissed. She said that I was right about coming out and that she didn't want to be without me. That night we went to bed for the first time. She didn't stay the night; and she was so funny, jumping into bed with all her clothes on. Rather than just take off her trousers and jumper, it was a while before she even removed all her clothes, which was rather strange, making love without the complete closeness. She told her landlady first about us and she said that she already knew that Dee was seeing someone and that it was no surprise to her that she was gay. In fact after coming out we all became friends and her landlady would quite often call round and have coffee with us. She was a nice person and I got on really well with her.

I think the worst bridge to cross was telling our parents. We decided mine should know first and I rather forced the issue on them. They asked me to take them to York one day and, as Dee was on her way to see her mother up the York Road, I asked if I could give her a lift. My mother said no, but for once I stood up to her and said that whether they liked it or not I loved Dee and if she couldn't come in the car, then they would have to find a new driver.

So Mother agreed and she even chatted to Dee on the way to her house, but I knew that something was up. Mother never accepted anything I did or any friends that I had and it wasn't likely to change. Nothing much was said to me for the rest of the journey, in fact my parents hardly spoke to me and when they did it was only to say how long they would be in York. I pointed out that my son would be coming home from school and I would need to be back for him.

My father's response to that was the fact that I should have made provisions for him before I left. How could I have done? I hadn't known that they wanted to go out until after my son had left for school. My father cursed and hollered about how stupid I was, how my son ruled my life and how now, to crown it all, I was with a woman. He called me a disgrace. I didn't say anything. There was no point as it would only turn even nastier. The journey home was slightly strained. The conversation was nonexistent, and though I expected it after telling them about Dee, I guessed there would be more to come sooner or later.

I didn't really care as I had my son and now I had what I always felt that I wanted: a woman. Moreover, she loved *me*. I couldn't work out why, she was only twenty years old and I was now thirty-three, I was sure she could do better than me. I wondered how her day was going. She was supposed to be telling her parents too. I hoped they didn't react too badly as it was me who forced the issue in the first place. I wouldn't see her until the next day as I had to do my shift at the fish shop and she was going to spend the night at her parents' and she hadn't transport to get back that evening.

Christopher was a little bit resentful of having to share me with someone else as he was used to having me all to himself, but he was a good chap. I explained to him that most children had a mammy and daddy, but then some people were different and women loved women and men loved men like Uncle Edward, I tried to make him understand in simple terms, but he seemed to grasp it.

He was still having night terrors and it led to him seeing a children's shrink, who seemed more concerned with my love life than anything else. She said that it was bad for my son to sleep with me when he was upset, as it would give him a mother fixation as regards sex when he grew up.

I thought that was a load of rubbish and if my son was upset and needed me then he could come into my bed. I still monitored the TV programmes he watched and they put him on a course of tablets and explained that it was just one of those things that some children had.

I was pleased about that because I had thought it was my fault and that I was a bad mother. It didn't help much when Mother insisted that the way I was living my life was having an effect on my son. I knew that wasn't true because the night terrors had started before Dee and I were involved.

Dee arrived back from her parents at two in the morning and knocked on the door to let her in. She said that she wanted to be with me and couldn't stop thinking about me, and that was why she came back without waiting for a lift from her parents. She said that she hadn't had the courage to tell her parents about us and that it didn't really matter as she wasn't living with them. I pointed out to her that they were bound to find out through the grapevine and surely it would be better coming from her, but she said she would cross that bridge when she came to it. There was no point in going on about it as she would only have a mood and I couldn't deal with that as she was so childish then.

She spent the rest of the night with me, but she still wasn't getting properly undressed. If I pushed the issue, or told her that I wanted to be closer to her, she would say that it was up to her to take the lead. If I kept on about it she would get up and go home. I really had a job understanding what she was thinking. I never worked her out all the time I knew her.

It was all rather silly really as she would be paying her lodge at the place were she was supposed to live, but she was almost living with me.

One evening I opened the door and her mother was on the doorstep. She said she wanted to see her daughter; of course, I invited her in, owing to the fact that Dee wasn't home from work yet. She refused and said she would wait in the car until Dee came home. Her choice I suppose, but she couldn't say I didn't offer.

When Dee did get in, I thought that I could warn her about her mother being outside, but I didn't get the chance; her mother was just behind her. The first thing that her mother said to her was, 'You. Out. Now.' Dee said she wasn't going, that she wanted to be with me. The next thing her mother was dragging her out of the door, I tried to get her mother off her and she turned on me. She said that if she had two bitches like us, she would have them put down; that stuck in my mind and for a while when we were in bed it would upset me. Dee was very understanding and patient about it.

Dee's mother accused me of seducing her daughter, saying that she wouldn't leave without her daughter. Dee repeatedly told her she wasn't going, but she wouldn't have it. I went to the next door neighbours and phoned the police and told them that I wanted someone removed from my home as she kept refusing to leave after I had repeatedly asked her to go.

When the police came Dee's Mother asked him what he thought of two women sleeping together and how would he like it if it was his daughter. Dee and I thought he was very understanding; he told her mother that it had nothing to do with him or her for that matter, all she had to do was leave my home. If she refused he would have to take her away and lock her up for the evening. Of course she went after that. The policeman said that the best thing to do would be to take out a court injunction to keep her away from the house, and Dee agreed. I was surprised that she did, as her mother, like mine, could always get round her.

It was creeping up to Dee's twenty-first birthday and I bought her a gold cross on a chain. The night after I gave it to her she seemed to change and went very quiet. On asking her if I had done something wrong she said that she thought we were both getting too serious and that we maybe shouldn't see each other so much. I couldn't work out what brought that on, but later found out that she had seen her mother earlier that day.

It wasn't too long before Dee moved into a flat about five hundred yards from where I lived. It turned out that her mother had paid the deposit and set her up in the flat as long as she kept away from me. Well if that was how she wanted it, what could I do? At least she wouldn't be walking past my house every lunchtime and evening. Of course I was upset and it hurt like hell; when she went against her mother with the injunction then I thought we had made it and no one else could come between us. It just goes to show how wrong you can be, she sure as hell didn't love me as I loved her. If she had, nothing or no one would have come between us.

She lasted about a week before she started walking round past my house again and looking to see if I was there. I didn't want to play her games, I figured it was time she grew up. As usual she knocked on my door one night and asked if I wanted to go round to her place one night for a coffee. She said that she had missed my company. I didn't give anything away, but played it cool although my heart was racing. I wouldn't let her know how I felt. Maybe that was the problem all through the relationship I never let her know exactly how I felt because then I thought she could hurt me if she knew my feelings. What an idiot I was.

Christopher and I went down a couple of evenings later. I thought if he went with me I wouldn't fall straight into her arms like the last time she had left me. He played with his toys while she took me round the flat and before long she had me. What can I say except that once she did, I was like putty in her hands, but I had to be strong. She had her place and I had mine and I couldn't and wouldn't live with this leaving and coming back. After that night she started coming round my house again, and of course we were nearly back to square one again. Then she made a decision, she would give up the flat and come to live with me and we would start off as a proper couple. I had to make sure that this was really what she wanted; I couldn't go through her leaving again. She seemed sure and didn't care any more what her mother or the outside world said, we could face it together.

XIV

So started another chapter in my life.

I would get up in the morning and cook the breakfast and then see her off to work and my son off to school, then go on my window-cleaning round. I would come home of a lunchtime now that Dee came home for lunch, sometimes we wouldn't even get any lunch, but go to bed instead. She was still slightly funny about removing her clothing, but it was getting better all the time, and I hoped that one day she might get there.

I would finish my round at three and get home ready for Christopher to come in, then clean the house and get the dinner ready for when Dee came home. On the nights that I wasn't at the fish shop she would work overtime and the nights that I worked she would babysit. She often said that my son was very awkward when she had to look after him, though naturally I wouldn't believe it and thought that Dee was just being nasty.

One evening I stopped outside the front door to listen. Sure enough, Christopher was being awkward, I could hear him throwing the cushions off the sofa and saying to Dee that she couldn't tell him what to do as it wasn't her house and she wasn't his parent. Well, I marched straight back in and told him that he had to behave himself or he'd have me to deal with. When I returned from the fish shop that evening Dee said that I was too soft with him and I should have given him a good hiding. She could never understand why I didn't belt him, but after the way I had being brought up, I would never do that to him.

The trouble was it was sometimes like having two children as Dee was very jealous about my son. She would call him my 'darling son' and say how he could never do any wrong, which wasn't true – he would get grounded and have his toys taken away for a week or whatever if he misbehaved. He would get a slap now and then, but I would never give him a good hiding.

Anyway I felt that things had to be talked about because, as much as I loved her, I couldn't go on as we were, as I felt that I was being used. She would come in of an evening take her dinner which I always had ready and pick the paper up, walk into the living room and turn the box on. After we had eaten I would clear away the pots and make a drink she would sit in front of the box all night and hardly say a word. Yes, we would cuddle up on the sofa, but if I tried to talk to her about anything she would shut off.

That night I knew that something had to be sorted out both financially and as regards the housework. We both worked so I figured that we should both share things work-wise at home and I made that suggestion to her. That went down like the *Titanic*. She refused to discuss it further and accused me of being too demanding. Why couldn't she talk about anything? Why would she just fly into a mood? I could never understand her as regards her attitude.

I went to bed first that evening and expected her to follow later, but no, she slept downstairs and hardly spoke the next morning, it was the first morning that I didn't get a kiss goodbye. I hated unpleasantness at the best of times, but more so between the two of us and I couldn't see any reason for it really, all we had to do was talk.

She came home at the usual time and she had bought me a big bunch of flowers and she walked in with that silly lopsided grin that used to make me melt, and said that I was right and she was sorry that she had been awkward. We agreed that we would share the housework on the weekends and she would help in the evening, she really enjoyed doing things once she got started and she was very good with anything manual so she took over the gardening and all the outside jobs.

When we could get a babysitter we would go out with Dee's old landlady and her husband for a drink or we would go to the pictures. The thing that I didn't like was the fact that her landlady and husband could hold hands in the pub or kiss or whatever. We couldn't do anything like that and sometimes I found it very frustrating having to keep my distance and Dee said she felt the same. We would on occasions walk down an alley just to kiss or have a cuddle, the trouble with that was once she kissed me I would want to make love. I couldn't help myself; as soon as her body came anywhere near me I was lost.

I remember the day we went on an outing with Dee's landlady and her five kids. It was only to the seaside, but the fact that no one knew us made a difference to Dee and she held my hand on the way there. She bought this stupid hat that said 'kiss me quick' on it and would torment me, knowing that I couldn't do anything, but it was all in fun. Christopher loved it with all the rest of the kids and he stayed with them while we went for a walk round.

On the way home in the bus we sat really close and held hands, I felt really happy and thought it was one of the best days we had ever had together. We arrived home about nine, I settled my son into bed while Dee took the dog for a quick walk and then the rest of the night was ours. We had a really loving night, just sitting in front of the coal fire listening to music, kissing, touching, making love, talking about the way we felt about each other. I said that I never wanted to lose her as I felt like I had waited all my life for her. The trouble, for me, was the age gap. Dee said that it wasn't important, but I thought fourteen years between us was too much and seemed a problem. So we drifted along like any couple, and before we knew it we had being together two months. She still wouldn't remove all her clothing at bedtime, which I found very strange; it was like a barrier between us. I loved her *so* much and wanted to be close to her body, but if I said anything she would turn off sexually and refuse to discuss it.

It was me that forced the issue. One day she was in the bath and I wanted the toilet so I asked her to unlock the door. I said I couldn't wait and she had to let me in. She opened the door and in I went. She said that she was sure I could have waited and she wasn't comfortable with it and that I just wanted to see her naked. I told her she had a wonderful body and asked why she would want to hide it from me; now that I had seen her I thought it was pointless. Finally the truth keep out. The fact of the matter was that if she removed all her clothing she would feel like she had given everything and then she couldn't get out of the relationship. Well, you can imagine how I felt. She was more or less telling me that she had thought about getting out of the relationship by holding back, I had thought we were happy and that she loved me as much as I loved her.

She said that she was rather frightened about the way she felt, and thought that it was too serious between us. I told her that I thought it was serious, but if she was frightened about committing to me then we should part now before it went any further. I had to leave her to think that one out; I knew I couldn't talk it through with her as she just wouldn't talk. A couple of days later she came in just as I was doing the dinner in the kitchen. She came up behind me, wrapped her arms round me and asked if I would marry her. I thought that she had lost it because two women couldn't get married, but Dee had bought a paper called *The Gay Times* and in it were married couples of the same sex.

Marriage wasn't recognised in this country, but it was in some countries abroad, but the whole point of it was a commitment between two people who loved each other. You can imagine how delighted I was. *She* wanted to spend the rest of her life with *me* or so she felt at that time. I said that there was nothing that I would like better, but thought that she should really think about it and make sure that was what she really wanted.

That night was the first night that she took all her clothing off and we made love, I mean really made love; the difference was unbelievable, I'd never felt so close to one person in all my life as I did that night. The way I felt that night was the way I wanted to feel for the rest of my life, she had her moods that was true, but as a lover she was thoughtful, considerate and would always try to please me.

I couldn't believe that six months had passed. We had our ups and downs, that much was true, but through it all we survived. Dee talked about us getting a car. My parents still had theirs, but I was still playing chauffeur to them, and they wouldn't let me borrow the car at all. So we bought an old Ford Escort and my parents weren't very happy about that.

They had accepted Dee as my partner in one way, but if anything was said to anyone outside the home, Mother would describe her as my friend. Mother tried to split us up several times by telling Dee untrue tales about me and usually men as she knew that Dee couldn't accept my past life very well. We had several arguments after she had been over to my mother's, but had to try and make her see that Mother was only trying to stir things up between us. It was hard, I didn't want to tell her much about my upbringing, she had to judge my parents for herself.

I still had my window-cleaning round; in fact, it was quite heavy going sometimes, I now had a lot of people on my books. I thought about giving it up, as that plus the fish shop was getting too much for me, but what with having to support my son, and Dee only giving me lodge money, I couldn't really afford to pack anything in.

Christopher had stopped his night terrors now so he was OK to be left of a night with a babysitter. I wished Dee and he could have got on a bit better. Sometimes I felt like piggy in the middle, of course I would always take my son's side, which didn't go down very well. It was all so childish and upsetting. If I bought him some sweets, I had to buy Dee some as well. It was like having two kids sometimes, if I bought him some new shoes it was like World War Three broke out and she would start saying that he was spoilt. The arguments that we had were mostly about my son and Dee's jealousy; sometimes she was really good with him and had more patience then me. I couldn't work it out, in fact after a while I stopped trying.

Though I loved both of them, Christopher always had to be first, as he relied on me for everything. Dee was a grown-up – or supposed to be – sometimes I wondered. We had had some nice days out after we bought the car. I would pack up a picnic and we'd go off and find a place near the water where Christopher would be able to play and we could just relax and enjoy being together as the places we found were usually pretty isolated.

I didn't see very much of the family considering that we only lived five doors away from them. I think Dee probably saw more of them than me as she would go over and chop my mother's sticks and do the garden for her as she thought it was disgusting that my mother had to do such jobs with grown-up men in the house.

That was the masculine side of Dee coming out. She would never let a woman do any heavy work, and when we went shopping she would insist on carrying it all and unload it out of the car herself, which sometimes caused problems between us. I didn't believe in playing to roles. I was neither butch nor femme.

I was just a woman who liked other women.

However, Dee believed in these labels and she would get moody if I stepped out of the role she had placed me in, the little housewife and homemaker. What she seemed to forget was the fact that before I met her I had to be both Mam and Dad and do everything myself.

I found it nice that she wanted to look after me, but felt that she wanted to change me into something that I wasn't. The only place that I was really femme was in the bedroom. Dee always took command there and I was very happy with my life in that department as she was a very considerate and thoughtful lover and taught me more ways to enjoy my body then I ever thought about or knew existed.

Time seemed to be flying by and before we knew it our first Christmas together was approaching. I had already bought Dee some clothes and hidden them away. When she came to live with me she really didn't have anything to wear if we went out, and the things she did have had seen better days. She wasn't one for caring about her appearance in those days, perhaps because no one had bothered about her, so when she did get something new she would wear it and wear it.

She loved it when we put the tree up and started decorating the house, I don't know who was more excited, her or my son! She said that in her home when she was growing up they only ever had second-hand things and she never looked forward to Christmas, especially when the other kids at school talked about what they had received – she had used to make it up about her presents.

So this Christmas would be very special for us all: Dee because it would be her first as a family unit, me because there had always been just my son and me and now I had someone to share all the things that made Christmas *Christmas*.

We went off on a bus trip, just Dee and I to do the shopping, it was lovely to have someone to choose the gifts with. Dee was like a child let loose in a toy shop it was wonderful to see her so happy. When it came to getting Christopher's presents I expected her to be funny about the amount of gifts he got, but she kept picking things up saying how we should buy him this. If she had been let loose she would have spent a fortune, but seeing as the money part was down to me, I had to put my foot down on some things.

That's another thing that I found funny about our relationship, the fact that her money belonged to her after she had paid me her 'lodge', as she called it. I thought as a couple we would pool our wages all together then together pay whatever had to be paid, but no; hers was hers and mine was mine.

My mother wasn't very happy that Christmas, as Dee and I wanted to cook the dinner at our own home since it was our first Christmas together. We spent Christmas Eve wrapping and sorting out the presents, and we agreed that we didn't want to go out for a drink, but that we would go New Year's Eve. She wanted to do the Father Christmas bit for Christopher, in other words, place his presents on the bottom of his bed for morning.

She liked all the clothes that I had bought for her, but didn't seem to know how to be pleased, so you were left with the thought, *Did she really like the things or was she just saying so?* She had taken great care with the presents she bought me, like remembering that I had liked a record advertised in the year or that I had said I liked something in a shop, all the presents were bought especially for me. She had bought me a box of Terry's All Gold because the ad said, 'See the face you love light up with all gold'. It was really sweet, but I didn't have the heart to tell her I didn't like dark chocs.

So began a new year. We seemed settled and happy; of course we had our disagreements as Dee still wouldn't talk things over, but would rather sulk about whatever the problem was.

She came in one evening and seemed to be on a right high, we all ate and then got Christopher settled down for the night. She and I took our coffee through to the living room and settled down for the evening. It was real cosy snuggled up on the sofa just in the firelight. Then Dee took something out of her pocket and showed it to me: a set of rings, an engagement and wedding ring. She put her arms around me and once again asked me to marry her. Although I still had a problem with the age difference I agreed, after all we had been together nearly a year and I didn't ever want to lose her.

We decided that now Christopher was older and no longer having nightmares I could pack in the window-cleaning round and get a proper job, with regular hours and a regular income. I saw a job advertised in the local paper for a supervisor at a dog food packing plant. Dee thought that I was above myself applying for a supervisor's job, but I had managed the fish shop often enough and my boss from there gave me a glowing reference.

I attended the interview on the day after phoning in, it seemed they were desperate for a supervisor to control the staff. When I arrived the boss's daughter told me that the manager was still out on business, but he wouldn't be long and she could take me round the place if that was OK by me. The manager was still not back after I had been round the place so she took me back to the office and asked if I would like a coffee while I waited and that she hoped I didn't mind waiting. Then the phone rang, and what she didn't realise was I could hear everything that was said on the phone. The person on the other end said that she should step away from me as she might get attacked owing to the fact that I was a lesbian. I didn't really know what to do about the phone call so I just chose to ignore it and wait for the manager.

The manager duly returned, and after a conversation with him he told me to phone him up in two days time. *Fat chance*, I thought.

Well, I phoned up a couple days later, thinking I wouldn't get the job, and to my surprise he asked me if I could start on the Monday. I wondered if I would get any hassle from the staff because of me being gay. I reckoned my best option was to go in as supervisor and forget anything that had been said, and just deal with it if it came up.

The girls, and that's all they were, resented having a supervisor, so my first step was to get them to train me. I figured it would make them feel good knowing that I was the new girl, so to speak. Once I had so much under my belt I would let them know that I was no fool and wasn't taking any nonsense off them. If they played fair by me then I would be fair with them; and I never asked them to do anything that I wouldn't do myself.

You always get one smart alec in the bunch and before long I had to speak to the manager about her not pulling her weight, so she resented me pretty much immediately. And so the cracks about gays started coming, stuff like having to wash cups carefully because of AIDS. Then one of the lads started on about having two women in bed at the same time, lesbians. I kept my cool and didn't rise to it, just ignored them.

The next day I had planned to get in a bit later, owing to my son having a dental appointment, so informed the girls that I knew how long it took to pack a box and that I expected eight boxes packed when I came in. Well, when I did get there the amount that had been packed wasn't worth mentioning, so I told them that they had better work extra hard from now on or they would be looking for employment. I told them from now on there had to be a certain amount packed each day.

Of course Miss Cocky had to start, didn't she, going on about how the night before there had been 'some poofs' in the pub and how they had all ended up taking the mickey. She looked straight at me when she said this so I thought it was time to clear some things up. I just looked right back at her and said that my brother was a homosexual and a good person. Of course she was all apologetic, but deep down she couldn't care less, it was just the fact that if I complained about her she wouldn't have a job. I then said that I knew that they were aware of the fact that I was also gay and we might as well get it all straightened up now, then maybe we would get some work done. I told them that my private life had nothing whatsoever to do with them as it didn't interfere with my work, and perhaps the subject could be closed with no more wisecracks. After that things settled down and they buckled down to work. There was only one member of staff that had to be dismissed, but that was more because he was incapable of doing the job than anything else.

The next thing that went wrong was the old Escort packed up and it needed far too much money spent on it to put it back on the road, but I needed a car to get to my job. I wondered if Father would let me borrow the Volvo, after all, it only sat there in the drive. It would do it good to be driven. Father surprised me by asking if I wanted to own it. If I was interested then I could buy it off him in instalments like I did with the washer. It was a lot more than the price of a washer and I didn't know if I wanted to take a big debt on like that. I said I would think about it and ask Dee what she thought.

We talked it over that evening, she said that at least I knew the car and that it had just had a thousand pounds spent on it and that was all my father was asking for it so really I couldn't go wrong, and that's how I ended up with a pretty decent car.

Life seemed pretty good. I had my son whom I loved to bits, a nice car, a good job and someone to love me. It was the last part that I sometimes just couldn't believe. I always thought that it wouldn't last, that she would get sick of me and move on because there was so much of an age gap between us.

Mother still tried to get at me, but she had new tactics: she would try to use my son against me, but thankfully it didn't work. I took him over to her house one morning so she could see him off to school, but instead of sending him to school she took him up to town and bought him a new winter coat. She said that his was a disgrace. Well I knew that it wasn't, it was just a bit old, so all she did was to save me buying a new coat for winter.

Three months had passed and Dee was starting to seem unsettled. She said that she wanted to go out more. I pointed out that by the time I had finished work, the last thing that I wanted to do on an evening was go out. The age gap was showing, just like I knew it would.

We had become friendly with a couple that lived just four doors away. Patrick worked with me and I took him into work a few mornings when his car was out of action so we started going out on the weekend with them. It wasn't really what I wanted to do with my spare time, and it seemed to me that their idea of fun was to go round the pubs until they were legless.

Apart from thinking it was a waste of money, I just hated feeling so ill the next day. Dee said that I was a misery guts and that I had to have all my own way and spend all my time with my precious son. It was true I suppose, it's just that I thought we were a family now and the weekends were the only time we had to spend all together. I said that if she wanted to go out with Patrick and his wife it was OK by me, but I didn't want to go boozing every weekend. I hoped that she wouldn't go out really, but it was her choice and there was nothing that I could do if that's what she wanted.

I worried that we were drifting apart and didn't know what to do about it. Even our sex life had tapered off. She would say that she was too tired, but she never seemed too tired to go out with Patrick and his wife. She started going down to their house of a night taking the chess board, she'd say that she went to play chess with the eldest son as I couldn't play the game. I told her that she could teach me to play and then we would see more of each other, but she just accused me of being possessive and wanting her to be with me all the time. She told me that I had to give her a bit of space.

I asked her if there was something going on between her and Winnie. Of course she wasn't, she said, Winnie was a married woman with five children. I put the idea out of my mind. I knew that Winnie had a boyfriend who visited when her husband was at work, so it didn't seem likely that she would go off with Dee, yet something wasn't right between us.

One night I made the first move in the bedroom department which I never did, as Dee liked to make all the moves, but she hadn't bothered with me so I felt that something had to be done. It didn't seem to get me anywhere; there wasn't any response out of her. In fact, what she did say really hurt me, she said that the scars on my leg were putting her off. They had never seemed to bother her in the past, I didn't know what to do. I felt like I was walking on eggshells. I couldn't say nor do anything right and I knew that Dee wouldn't talk about the problem. She claimed that it was all in my head and things were OK, which we both knew wasn't true. We had drifted too far apart.

One day, out of the blue with no warning, she came home and said that she was leaving me as she didn't love me any more and it was pointless pretending. I'm ashamed to say that I begged and pleaded with her to tell me why, surely we could work it out, I would do anything for her, she just had to tell me what. She wouldn't even listen to me. Instead she got out my tablets and a bottle of brandy and said that the best thing for me to do was end it all because she didn't care what I did.

She took the things that she had packed and said that she would come back later for the rest of her stuff, she would let me know when. I didn't know what to do. I felt like there was nothing left, even my son didn't compensate for the deep loss that I felt.

XV

My son had always meant everything to me, but right then I couldn't think and what I did the next night, as far as I was concerned, was unforgivable.

He came in from school and I can't even remember what he said to me, but it certainly didn't warrant my reaction. I took him and threw him through the door into the house, poor little lad didn't know what had hit him, I had never treated him like that.

I felt so sorry for my treatment of him, but I had done it and I could never take my actions back, I cried for him to forgive me. Of course he said it was OK, but it scared me that I had done that to my son. *Me*, who swore that I would never beat my child and I had done just that, right then I hated Dee for what she had driven me to.

I took my son over to my mother's and said that I couldn't deal with him right now. Well of course I got what I had expected from my mother. She said that it was unnatural that two women should live like that and she knew it wouldn't last and if I didn't pull myself together they would take me away as being insane. Maybe she was right, all I knew was that I couldn't eat or sleep and that when I did sleep I could see Dee standing under the lamp like she used to in the early days.

I went to work, but couldn't really concentrate on the job. I kept asking myself where I had gone wrong, why she didn't love me any more.

I still worked with Patrick, and one night Winnie, his wife, came down to see me. She said that if she could help in any way she would. Any thought I had about there being something between Dee and her disappeared, she wouldn't be consoling me if it was all her fault.

I had only left my son at my mother's for one day and night, but I felt that my arm had been cut off without him being near. We had never being apart since he was born and it wasn't his fault the way things were, so I brought him home.

I saw Dee nearly every day as she went down to Winnie's every night. She had a motorbike, which she had bought off my brother, and I could see it parked outside Winnie's every night until late. The trouble was that Winnie lived opposite my mother so I had to see Dee every night. I never saw her to speak to as she soon disappeared down Winnie's path, but it was heartbreaking seeing her and knowing that I would never be kissed or held by her again. It was only my son that kept me going, but the nights were the worst when he was in bed and I was left with my thoughts and memories.

About a week after we had split up, Winnie left her husband and he started telling me how when I went to work on a morning Winnie would go to my house and take things – bread and sticks, anything that would save her spending the housekeeping money. Talking to Patrick, who was just as cut up as I was, was good for both of us. He said that the children wanted new shoes and there was no food in the house as Winnie had being saving the money to go away with Dee. It seemed that Patrick and I were the only ones that didn't know what was going on, all the neighbours knew what the crack was.

Why couldn't she have told me the truth when I asked her if there was anything going on between her and Winnie? If she had told me perhaps I wouldn't have kept asking myself what I had done wrong. But then it must have been my fault, perhaps if I had gone out with her when she wanted me to instead of worrying about money, she wouldn't have left me. I degraded myself by going to her workplace and asking her if we couldn't start again and things would be different. All she said was if I didn't leave her alone she would see someone about stopping me pestering her, what could I do?

One of her workmates told me that she had handed in her notice and she had a ticket to go on the bus to London on Friday evening at midnight. *If I could talk to her then I'm sure things would be all right.* I asked my brother if he would drive me up to see her before she got on the bus, but to, please, not tell my mother. My sister looked after my son and off we went. We saw her get on the bus and make her way down to the back. She was by herself, I hoped and prayed it wasn't true about Winnie. Surely she would have been there with her, right?

I tried to kid myself that she was only going away for a break and then she would be back. We followed the bus for about six miles. I cried my eyes out all the time, and Dee, well all she did was put her two fingers up at us. *How can someone be like that?* After all that had gone on between us I couldn't understand any of it. My brother really didn't know what to do with me, he turned round and took me back home, all the while I sobbed my heart out. When I got home he went for my mother as he didn't know how to deal with me – as if she would help me. All I got off her was, 'Pull yourself together', otherwise she threatened to get the doctor and he would put me away. According to her I was behaving like an insane person. I told her to leave me alone, I didn't need her ranting at me, but she didn't understand.

I did end up going to the doctor's though. I couldn't cope. He put me back on the antidepressants, which helped a bit, but it was hard going to work and coming in to no one. My brother Edward really came through for me though, he took me out to a gay club to keep my mind off things. At least he tried, but I didn't want to know anyone, it was pretty much a waste of time. I don't think anyone ever realised what I felt for Dee.

She had been gone for about three weeks when a letter arrived from her. Of course I thought that she had changed her mind and wanted to come home, but on opening it I discovered it was a postcard with a gorilla. The inscription said that it reminded her of me. Why did she have to be so cruel? It wasn't the only thing I received from her either. One day a parcel arrived with a vibrator and a note saying that that was all I needed now.

I had been off work for a month as I couldn't stand going in. Patrick was there and there were too many memories, so I got a new job at a garage as a forecourt attendant. I was able to keep myself occupied learning the job, and that left me only with the nights. I tended to keep my son up later than usual, but after he retired I felt lonely and stupid that I had let someone hurt me like she had. I vowed that I would never give my all to anyone again.

Time was a healer. Six months passed and suddenly I didn't think of her as much. Perhaps I had simply tried (and succeeded) to alter my life so that there was only me and Christopher going out to places with the little dog, thank God for them.

My brother took me out again and although I wasn't looking for anyone this woman came over and asked if she could buy me a drink. It was flattering as there were lots nicer looking women than me in the club. Her name was Babs and she told me a bit about herself. She seemed like a nice person, but the last thing I wanted was to get involved with anyone, nice or not.

She sat with us all night and in spite of myself it was nice having someone to talk to who understood the relationship, or rather the break-up of two women, she had gone through a break-up the year before and she said that things did get better. I said she should look me up if ever she was in my neighbourhood, although the chances of that were pretty slim as she lived in the big city of London. Little did I know where that night would lead.

About a month later I was going to my mother's one evening as she wanted to see me about taking them somewhere at the weekend. Walking along on the other side of the road was this person; I didn't recognise her till she got a bit closer, and even then I had a job placing her. It was Babs. Well, I had told her to look me up if she was ever in the area! And here she was, taking me at my word.

She was a very attractive woman and there wasn't any doubt that I felt something for her. She was slim with blue eyes and blond hair, but most of all she was two years older than me. There was only one problem: it was a two-bedroom house, three-bedroom really, but my son had the smallest room as a play room so it was full of his toys.

I felt strange as she was a complete stranger to me, after all she could be a mass murderer or something really, but she got on very well with my son and he seemed to like her so that was something. She asked if she could stay for a few days as she was between jobs and she was thinking of moving anyway, as she wanted to get away from the city. I told her that I had to go to work early the next morning as I did shift work and this week I was on earlies. I also said that I would sleep on the sofa as there was a lack of beds. She replied that there wasn't any need for anyone to sleep on the sofa. We were adults and it would be OK for her to share my bed as she wouldn't attack me, but she said it all with a laugh so I felt completely safe with her.

The biggest problem was my mother. Trying to tell her that someone was staying with me at the moment would go down like a ton of bricks, even more so if she knew Babs was a gay woman. Mother said that she didn't want to know, that I was making a complete fool of myself and she didn't want to meet her. In fact she said that she would disown me if I was going to continue this lifestyle.

When I returned from work the next day I walked into a lovely clean house and a fire burning in the grate and the supper was all prepared. Babs said that she hoped I didn't mind her doing all that, but seeing as I had been at work all day then I wouldn't want to work when I came in. I began to think I could get used to that kind of treatment and coming home to someone waiting for me.

She asked me if I wanted to get a babysitter and she would take me out for a drink that evening. Of course, I immediately began thinking about where I thought I had gone wrong with Dee. I didn't want to make the same mistake again. We just went down to the local pub at the end of our street, but I felt really good. No one knew her and she was with me when, with her looks, she could have anyone she wanted. There was no moodiness with her, and we had a real laugh as she had a great sense of humour.

Babs had been staying at my house for six days when she said that she must get back to her flat and let them know where she was and what was happening. She then asked me if I would like her to return so that we could start out together as a couple. My son liked her and they seemed to hit it off and she was a really attractive lady and I felt flattered that she wanted to move in with me. It was nice having someone to come home to after work and cuddle up to of an evening. She had not pushed me for anything else in the bedroom and I must say that really I was rather disappointed on that front. I thought that maybe I didn't turn her on that way, after all I wasn't nothing special and Dee had said that my scars had put her off. Maybe it was the same with Babs.

I hadn't known what sex was all about until I had met Dee.

She had taught me that you could get satisfaction by yourself, which you could, but it was nothing compared to the real thing, it just helped to relieve the frustration. But the feeling of a passionate kiss and the closeness of two people touching and being naked and just wrapped in each other's arms was something else altogether. I found that I missed the sexual part of a relationship, which rather worried me, as sex had never played a big part in my life before.

I took Babs to catch the bus on the Friday evening and she said that she would see me on the Monday. I wondered if she would return or have second thoughts once she got back to the bright lights, so to speak. After all there wasn't much here in this town to fetch anyone back.

My mother would still pass me in the street and not say a word, just look right through me. Silly really, as Christopher still went across to see his grandparents all the time and I knew that she asked him things about Babs and what went on in the house, as he would tell me when he came home. I didn't want him to be questioned by her, but there wasn't much I could do about it. She wasn't speaking to me and she didn't want Christopher to think that it mattered what he said to her.

I took Christopher out for a picnic that weekend, it was rather nice just him me and the dog. He asked if Babs was coming back as he liked her and she was a lot better then Dee. He said he had been pleased that Dee had left, but never said so till now as he knew that it hurt me.

Monday soon came round. I took Chris to school and then returned home to clean the house before the bus arrived. Deep down I didn't think she would be on the bus, but there she was sitting at the back of the bus as it pulled in. She got of the bus, threw her bag down and came straight to me and kissed me. I was shocked, but also delighted, she couldn't have cared less about what people said. She figured that people met with a kiss all over the world. Anyway people could think what they wanted as she didn't care, she wasn't ashamed of what she was and I certainly wasn't. It wasn't that she broadcasted the fact that we were lesbians, but if she wanted to kiss me or hold my hand then she would do so regardless of what people said or thought.

When we arrived home, she explained to Christopher that she liked his mam and that sometimes she would like to kiss me and she hoped that he would be all right with that as he could kiss me when he wanted. She treated him like a person and took his feelings into consideration and I liked that.

We ate and got Christopher settled down for the night then Babs opened a bottle of wine that she had brought with her. I wasn't really a drinker, but we shared the wine and went to bed, pretty early really, as I was on the early shift next day. Our relationship was still not on a sexual level, possibly, I thought, because she was waiting for me to make the first move. As much as I wanted to I found that I couldn't, I guess that Dee knocking me on that front had some affect on me, but I did cuddle up to Babs and that was all it took as far as she was concerned, she turned round and started touching me and kissing me and that was enough to get me going. When we made love it was wonderful, and after we lay in each other's arms and talked, something that I had never done with Dee. Babs said that if we didn't talk then we could carry on doing things that did nothing for each other. I must admit that Babs liked things that I had never even heard about, let alone done to another person.

I've found that as I've grown older, my relationship with Babs was not all I thought it to be. I find it difficult to remember now things as they once were, but looking back it seems that I really just fell into the affair with Babs without giving it too much thought at all. After all, I hardly knew the woman. I guess it was all down to the fact of my feeling lonely and unlovable, which wasn't really any excuse to go into another relationship, and thinking back it certainly wasn't fair to Christopher. But at that time all I cared about was getting over Dee and having someone new in my life who helped me do that. I did still think about Dee, but the ache and the longing that I felt before Babs came on the scene wasn't as bad as it had been. All I can say was that I didn't want to make the same mistakes with Babs that I thought I had made with Dee, so whatever Babs said or suggested I went along with. Rather stupid thinking back now.

I still didn't know that much about Babs even though she was now living with me and I was frightened about asking her anything. I figured that she would tell me what she wanted me to know in her own time. I knew that she had being in a long-term relationship and that is why she ended up in London. She had no commitments, which, thinking back, was very strange as we all have someone in our life or most of us have. She said she hadn't anyway and could come and go as she pleased, which was rather worrying as she could walk out on me any time she felt like it.

She did say that she had been married and was the mother of four children who were all grown up now, but she never said where they lived. Something should have twigged then because I would die for my son: I wouldn't – couldn't – leave him and would always want to be in touch with him, even when he had grown up. But it didn't seem as if she wanted to talk about her children so I just left it.

As for what she did for a living, she said that she had always been in the catering trade and had worked in a hotel in London, but she wanted a break from work right now and would go on sick leave. She had every reason to do so or so I thought(I didn't realise that she was working the system), as she had scars from heart surgery, once in South Africa and once in this country.

That's how I found out more about her family, as they were all still in South Africa; she had lived there with her husband and children. She told me that she had married young and had told her husband at the time that they wouldn't have a sexual relationship if she married him, which he had been all right about at the time. However, after getting married, he had forced himself on her one night. She had her first child from that and couldn't leave him as he was so sorry for what he had done. He worshipped his child and her also. She said that each child had been conceived the same way so she was tied to him.

After all that she started living her life as she wanted, having affairs with different women until she had met Alex whom she eventually left the country with. They bought a greengrocer's shop together in Norfolk and then she found her girlfriend with a man. Even though she forgave her, Alex had kept seeing his man until Babs couldn't accept it any more. She didn't want all the fighting about the business, so she walked away with just her personal things.

It had made her very bitter towards men and she said that at least she knew that I would never do anything like that with a man as she had seen my reaction to guys. At that, I believed anything she told me and never questioned anything, all that I thought about was not to make a mess of this relationship like I thought that I had done with Dee.

So, even if I didn't want to go out to the pub, if Babs wanted to do so I would go along without question. The money never even came into it. I still worried about the bills and groceries and everyday things, but I worried silently. Thinking back on my life with Babs then, I guess it wasn't all that I made it out to be, maybe I just didn't want to sound as if I was a failure with my relationships. Looking back on the situation now I guess none of them really worked out.

I came out one morning to see Chris off to school. Babs was still in bed, which was something that I would never let Dee do: if I was up she had had to be up also. But Babs and I had had a late night the night before.

I never accepted anything calmly and this was no exception – the car had been spray-painted by someone in the night. The words 'lesbians live here' had been sprayed I wasn't bothered about the wording just the damage to the car. I ran in and straight upstairs to Babs who calmly said that she would go have a look after we had a coffee and I had calmed down. She went out to see the mess on the car, came back in and took a Brillo pad out with her, I thought that would just scratch the car, but it actually took the writing off.

So we both went out armed with a bucket each and started to scrub the car. As we were involved in this my mother walked by. She actually spoke, though she might as well not have bothered. All she said was that we could expect that happening to us if we didn't live a normal life like everyone else. And what's normal? I still ask myself even now.

After we had cleaned, Babs said that I had to put on some 'clean drawers', as she put it, as she was taking me away from everything. We would go to York for a meal. Of course I never questioned why York, just asked if would we be back in time for Christopher leaving school. I didn't want him over at my mother's. She said that she had never known anyone worry so much about things, but of course we would be back for him.

If she had told me to lay down in the middle of the road I would have done so. It was like I hadn't a mind of my own at that time, as if I was under a spell. Thinking back now it was due to the fact that I was frightened of losing her, frightened of being by myself, the fear of just living life I suppose. After all, I had been by myself for seven years bringing up Christopher before I got involved with Dee, so what was my problem?

Babs never seemed to worry about anything, just spent money without thinking of the next day. She showed me a side of life that I had never known. Perhaps that was the attraction, she was so different to anyone that I had ever known. We spent three hours in the restaurant eating, but mainly drinking. She liked her drink. That was something that I had noticed about her, after a couple of glasses she would open up and talk about her past life and I believed everything that she told me.

We left York later than we had planned and if it boiled down to it I wasn't fit to drive the car, I had to have been over the limit. I drove like an idiot as far as I was concerned, but Babs said that I was a very good driver, which was very flattering. We just got home in time to see Christopher coming down the road.

Babs said that we could take him out and treat him, after all we had being out for a treat so he deserved one too. She knew that he wanted a pair of Doc Martin's and even though I wasn't keen on him having them she talked me round to letting him have them. She said that if I signed a cheque she could put the money in the bank in a couple of days' time and the cheque would take two days at least to clear. I had never signed a cheque if the money wasn't in the bank to cover it, but seemed to have been doing a lot of that since meeting Babs.

She also wanted some brandy from the off-licence at the same time, she said it would just round off our night. That was probably the first night that I didn't really agree with her. I never said any thing to her, but she could see that I wasn't very happy. Later on in the night as I said that I didn't want any more to drink as I had had enough for one day, I would sooner go to bed as I had to go to work the next day.

That night I saw another side of her and it was a side of her that I didn't like all. It was down to the drink, of course, but I had enough of that when I was growing up. Thank heavens Christopher was settled in bed. She just ranted on about me not being able to enjoy myself and I was turning into a right miserable sod. Then she started on about her past girlfriend and how things never went right in her life.

She eventually fell asleep on the sofa and for once I didn't want her to wake up. She could stay there for the night. She talked away in her sleep about past loves and you would think that she was with them the way she carried on. She pulled me down to her, but the last thing that I wanted was for her not to know who she was making love with, she then started spouting a load of double Dutch as far as I could make out.

I felt a lot of mixed emotions at that time – fear mostly, but I can't really say what I was frightened of. I went to bed and took Christopher in with me. I figured that if she woke up, she would sleep downstairs if she knew that Chris was with me.

She did wake up and came upstairs, still drunk and talking a load of rubbish. As far as I could tell she said that I was bloody stupid and that Chris had to go back to his own room. I asked her to go downstairs or said that I would go down as Christopher had woken up by this time and he was upset. There wasn't really much point in trying to talk sense to her as she wouldn't listen, so when she went down to the toilet I put a chair behind the door in case she came back upstairs. Of course she did and then started ranting and raving. I said that I would talk to her tomorrow when she was sober, but she wasn't getting in till then.

The music came on downstairs and she played that for about an hour then all went quiet. Christopher by this time had settled down again so I crept downstairs to see if Babs had settled down. What came next I never expected. She was sitting on the hearth with tablets all over the place and empty pill bottles. I tried to ask her if she had taken anything, but she just laughed and kept on drinking. 'What does it matter?' she slurred. Well of course it mattered, but I couldn't make her see that at all. I couldn't risk leaving her not knowing what she had taken so I woke up my next-door neighbour and asked her if I could use her phone to phone the doctor. Of course I had to tell her what had happened, but she was very understanding. I went back home and told Babs that the doctor would be coming so she had better tell me what she had taken. She answered that she hadn't taken anything. Did I think that she would be stupid enough to kill herself over any woman, she jeered. I tried to explain that I didn't want to fight, but was concerned about her. She just laughed.

When the doctor arrived she told her that she hadn't taken anything, but the doctor said that she had to go to hospital regardless. There was a chance that she had taken something and just wasn't saying. The ambulance arrived and off she went and I told her that I would come and see her next day. As she went out of the door all she said were two words: 'So butch'.

Of course, the next day no one knew what had happened except myself and the woman next door, but I guessed it wouldn't be long before everyone knew, that how it was in our town, not that I was bothered. I went to see Babs around mid-afternoon as I had to get back for Chris. I didn't really know what to say to her except to try to explain why I did what I did the night before. I tried to tell her that it was because my father had always drunk when I was a child and that it frightened me when someone got drunk and ranted on.

She apologised and said that it wouldn't happen again as she wouldn't be returning to the house. After what she had done she couldn't face anyone round there. She admitted as well that it had been mine and Dee's home and she couldn't cope with the fact that Dee and I had lived there together before she and I had met. She wanted us to start again somewhere else away from my parents and all the memories of Dee. I said that we would look for somewhere as soon as she came out, but no, she said that she wasn't returning until a new place had been found.

Of course I was upset and didn't know how to get round the issue, but she wouldn't budge on her decision, and when the hospital let her go the social worker from the hospital found her a flat in Darlow.

XVI

It was very easy for Babs as she hadn't much to move or much to walk away from as far as I was concerned. I went to visit her shortly after she moved and she said that I must understand that she did want to be with me, but not at the house where I was living. She wanted us to make a new start together. I suppose I could understand that, I wouldn't like to be where her past girlfriends had been.

The only way to do it was to see who was in the council offices on the exchange list and get a swap with the houses. Perhaps it would be better away from my parents and maybe the area. Thinking about it I realised that I had never had the nerve until now, but with someone beside me I could do it.

The council only had one person on the exchange list and that was in a little village about five miles out of the town, which was all right for me. I had transport, but it would depend on how Chris felt about it and if Babs liked the idea. I decided that I had better talk to my son about it first before telling Babs, because if he didn't like it then there would be no way that I would move. He had gone through enough after the break-up of my last relationship and he didn't need any more problems because of me.

Actually, he really surprised me. He seemed to be happy at the thought of setting up a new home with Babs. He was a quiet child who didn't make friends very easily, a bit of a loner really, and I figured the thought of a new school would have frightened him, but he didn't seem bothered by it at all.

We both went to see Babs to tell her and ask her how she felt about being away from the town and fairly isolated. She seemed pleased with the idea. So that was her and Christopher happy; even though I was OK with everything, I still had mixed emotions about moving. It was the fear about leaving everyone I knew, and I worried that being so isolated could end up being a problem; but if this is what it took to get away from the world I grew up in, and both Babs and Chris were both happy, then I would go along with it.

I phoned the people at the other house and arranged to go up and see it. I was so nervous, but there wasn't much point in planning anything until we had met each other. The next day, after Christopher had finished school, we all went up to see the house. It was a bit awkward as after I had picked up Chris, we then had to go and get Babs from her flat because she was still refusing to go into town. When we arrived at the house it turned out that I knew the woman who lived there. She had babysat for me before I had met Dee.

She had stuck in my mind as she had caused a few problems at the time. She had spread a rumour around that I had made a pass at her and that she could twist me round her little finger because of my feelings for her. To be honest, I hadn't helped matters. I bought her a bracelet I knew she liked for Christmas, but it just served to 'prove' what she had said about me. The thing is, that was the way I behaved with anyone. It gave me great pleasure to buy presents for others. Of course I knew that the whole thing was nothing more than a case of a young schoolgirl trying to be big and important with her friends. I would have ignored it, but my mother heard the rumour and, being my mother, believed there was something in it. Of course, she would.

I hoped the woman had forgotten about it, as it was several years ago. Fortunately, she already knew my house as her parents lived round the corner from me, which meant that it all depended on how we felt about her house.

It was a three-bedroom like mine, only the rooms were larger. It had a separate kitchen-cum-dining room, and an outside washhouse. The toilet was inside the house, which was smashing. The decor left a bit to be desired, it wanted doing from top to bottom, but the woman explained that they just wanted to move so hadn't bothered to fix the place up.

I don't want to come off like I'm being clever or anything, but my house was always immaculate. At that time I was very house-proud and cared where I lived and, more to the point, what I lived in. So I brought the state of the house up with Babs and she reminded me that she wouldn't come back to the house I was in at the moment and that this house would be ours. 'We can decorate it together,' she said. If that was what she wanted, it was OK by me.

The only problem was that Babs wanted the house in both our names and I wasn't sure if the council would go for that, but I knew it was the only way she would move in with me. Dee had always wanted me to do that as well, but I had refused because I always thought that if anything went wrong she would be able to claim half of everything and I had worked very hard for all that I possessed. I have learnt over the years that they are only material things and don't mean much at the end of the day, but then I guess back then it was very important to me having a lovely home. The fact that I had achieved it all *and* raised Christopher all by myself probably made it that much more important. I don't know.

Anyway, I told myself, one of the reasons that Dee had left me was because it was just my house. I had to remember that at the start of my affair with Babs I had promised that things would very different. I was determined not to make the same mistakes with her that I had made with Dee.

What I should have realised is that they were two different people. Dee never worried about taking anything, Babs. I found out later, would. What a hassle with the council to get the house in both our names. I ended up having to lie and say we had been together longer than we had, that we both wanted to make a start in our own home and that Babs would have more security if it was in both our names. They had never done that for same-sex relationships and they said they would have to have a meeting over it and we could have a decision in a week's time.

That was another week separated from her, but she agreed to come home with me as long as I didn't expect her to go out and I didn't tell anyone she was there. Of course I agreed that I would wouldn't. The week soon passed and we went to see what their decision was as regards both names. They had passed it and we had a moving date, as long as all parties agreed to sign that we had all seen both houses and we wanted them as they stood.

It was all on my shoulders as Babs needed to go back and pack her flat in. Christopher was very excited about the move and looking forward to starting his new school. We had already been down to the school and he had met some of his teachers. It was just a small village school and he had to catch a bus from our new home as the school was about five miles away, but he seemed quite happy about it.

We didn't tell anyone that we were moving, not even my mother. It hurt a little keeping silent, but then my family had never been bothered about me when I was just four doors away. I secretly hoped that this time I would be able to break away from them all. It was very hard work packing and driving the van from one house to another, but at last it cut the expense in half as they had agreed to pay half. Babs waited at the new house as we went back and forth between the two collecting our things. Christopher stayed with her, too. I figured at least she could get the beds up if nothing else.

It was hard for me to leave the old house, the memories and the family, as well as all the people I knew in the town. After ail I had been there for nearly thirty-seven years – all my life really. About the only person sorry to see me leave was the next door neighbour, but at least she knew who the new people were as they had grown up in the area. She said she would have rather had me stay, which was really kind of her.

If I had only known then what was in store I would never have left, but maybe it's just as well we don't know what life has in store.

It was exciting to have a new home to start decorating and making nice, the trouble was that there was no spare cash to do anything with. Babs said that we would do it together, starting at the top with Christopher's room and working our way down. She told me to stop fretting over it as it would all come right in the end; she said that I was worried over nothing. It was only that I was used to having carpet down and a nice home. She reminded me that it was our home now and not just mine, and that we would decide things together.

I'm not sure how happy I was about that, I have always done what I wanted in my home and answered to no one, but then I thought that was maybe where I had gone wrong with Dee. I didn't want this relationship to go wrong, so I went blindly along with whatever Babs said. Neither of us had a job, so that was the first thing on my mind, but Babs said that we would settle in before finding work. Except there wasn't much we could do, with no money coming in, the best we could do was keep it clean. So we started on the garden. It was rather large and very overgrown, but bit by bit we cut it all down so it was just one big lawn and that suited us both.

Babs said that she would sort out the bills if I gave her the dole money after I had bought the shopping and the cigs for us both. She told me what she wanted in the food line, as she said she could make a pound of mince go a long way as long as she had some other things to go with it. She needed 200 cigs a week and all I wanted was two ounces of baccy as I rolled my own cigs. We had a bit of a tiff about it really as I thought her cigs were an expense we could do without, but there was no way she was going to smoke roll-ups. She accused me of not caring about her, saying that her cigs were the only thing she had in her life to enjoy. She convinced me that I was in the wrong. She was very good with words and could manipulate things so that I came off sounding unreasonable and wrong. At that time it seemed like I was just getting to know her, so making up after the disagreement seemed well worth it all.

Christopher seemed really happy in his new school. He had made friends with the girl next door and she came over to his room to play and he went to her house to play. We had let him choose his own room in the house as Babs said that it would make him feel good and more settled. I must admit that she was much better with him than Dee had ever been and he really liked her, but that was perhaps due to the fact that she had been a mother. I could never understand how she could leave her children. Wild horses would never get me away from Christopher.

Every time I asked Babs about her life in South Africa she changed the subject or said that it didn't matter about her past, it was the future that mattered. As long as I loved her and wouldn't play around like her ex had then that was all she wanted. Slowly I found out little bits about her, like how her ex had played about with another man, which was why she had left her, plus the business they had had. She had walked away from it all.

As regards her kids, well she had given them a choice: go with her or stay with their father. She thought they were better off with him, as it seems she had been asked to leave South Africa and to never return, for what reason I do not know and still don't to this day.

One of the things I didn't like about the new place was the fact that the pub was just across the road. Babs used the excuse that we would get to know people quicker if we went over there, which I suppose was true, but I wasn't really bothered about knowing other people. I had her and my son and that was all that mattered to me. And I can't really say that she was a sociable type, she didn't like anyone to know what we were doing in the house or out of it.

She did want people to know that we were a couple, however, and let them know it by being a bit protective and showing affection. She would put her arm round me and that was very nice, but I did find it slightly embarrassing as I am sure other people did; yet in another way I felt pleased. All my life no one had ever shown me love and Babs made me feel loved and wanted.

So the weeks moved by and the only thing that seemed to get done was the garden. Babs wasn't one for working round the house. She said that she did the meals and it was down to me to do the rest. She didn't want me to go to work, so our money situation was far from good, but I didn't argue. I didn't want her to leave me. I found it hard to think that anyone could truly stay with me because they loved me, I couldn't see what they saw in me. To make matters worse, if I did argue, Babs had a way of making me feel like I was in the wrong. The trouble was all the money seemed to go on drinking across the way. It's not that I begrudged her any pleasure; it was just the fact that the house had no wallpaper, no carpets except for in the kitchen-cum-dining room. If only I could have just got on with painting at least one room then I would have felt happier about the place, but at that moment all I could feel was regret that I had left my old home.

Even though I didn't want to question Babs I had worked it

out that all my money went straight to her and her money also went to her and there wasn't much to show for it. I think this was the biggest argument that we had had so far and I wasn't willing to back down. She accused me of not trusting her, and said that all women were alike and just wanted something off her. She wasn't willing to discuss it, and went to the pub instead. When she returned she was well gone. If she thought that I would drop the issue, she had another think coming. I kept on going and got a slap or two for my trouble. There was no use trying to talk to her when she was in that state.

I wasn't willing to leave this issue and the next morning I pointed out that I had never been out of work and that I needed a job. She agreed and we sat down to work out how we both wanted the home to look. This was very strange for me as I had never consulted anyone as regards the home, I had always done it myself, but I saw this as another mistake I had made with Dee and so went along with how Babs wanted it.

In the local paper there was a job advertised at a café just down the road from where we lived, so I applied for it and was asked to start on the Monday, just three days time. This gave Babs a reason to go out and celebrate, not that she needed one. Still, I figured that now I was working maybe I wouldn't feel so confined and useless, plus there would be money to start working on the decor. Or so I thought.

The job was OK, it was just serving and clearing tables, nothing that I hadn't done before. The girls who I worked with were another matter all together. There were a couple of men who came in regularly who the girls called poofs. They would throw their cups and anything else they used straight in the bin after they cleared their table, saying they didn't want to catch AIDS off the 'dirty weird sods'. I wondered what they would think if they found out about me and Babs; we only lived down the road. You can you imagine how my life would be if that was how they felt about homosexuals.

I talked it through with Babs that evening. She was furious. She said that I wasn't to go there any more, she would phone and tell them that I was ill. I suppose that a couple week's wages were better than nothing. The trouble was I needed to save some money as Chris would be up at the 'big school' in another year and would need a new uniform.

Babs had other plans. She wanted to get the car resprayed and as my young brother worked at a garage she said it would be cheaper there so off we went to find out. The car did not want a new coat of paint, but she said that as we had a new house but couldn't have a new car, changing the colour would be just as good. As usual I went along with what she wanted, and I'll bet you're thinking that I didn't have a mind of my own, that it was always what Babs wanted. In a way you would be right. I went along with everything she asked because I didn't want to lose her. Once again I compared what had gone wrong with Dee and I wasn't about to go there again.

Babs arranged to get the car done and for us to have a car on loan till ours was ready. I should have guessed she was up to something when she told me when we got the loan car. She wanted me to drive her down to Norfolk where she had her clothes and things stored with a friend. She reasoned that petrol would be cheaper in the loan car. I was kind of excited with the idea, maybe I would meet someone who could tell me something about her. After all what did I know apart from what she had told me.

Driving down she was very happy because she would now have some decent clothes to go out in, and would have all her records and tapes back. I remember looking at her and asking myself what she saw in me. She was so good-looking and slim – beautiful as far as I was concerned. If ever I asked her she wouldn't answer me except to say that she had been with good-looking girls and that looks didn't matter. I must admit she didn't give me much of a boost with that answer!

We arrived at Norfolk and parked outside a shop. She told me to wait in the car a minute and went inside. She disappeared round the back and came back a few minutes later with a man and some bags. She introduced me as a good friend that had driven her down, thanked the chap and we left. Any ideas that I had about getting to know something about her were gone. She told me that he and his wife knew nothing about her being gay, which was why she introduced me as a good friend. It seemed like she had been a closet gay in Norfolk.

The things we had travelled all that way for consisted of a couple of bags. Of course I had to open my big mouth and say that I didn't think it was worth the journey or the petrol. That really upset Babs, she said that when she walked out of her home she had left everything except for these bags and in them were her designer trousers – I can't remember the make as I had never bothered about such things. Then she started on about where she had stayed on holiday with the ex – top hotels, etc. She said that she would take me one day. Am I stupid or what? It was another world to me, and I really believed that one day we would go there.

We arrived home about 3 p.m., just in time to pick up Christopher from school. Babs suggested we go out for a meal to celebrate her getting her things – when didn't we go out to celebrate I asked myself. I didn't dare to say anything to Babs just then, but decided that I wasn't going out all the time. There was still so much that we needed to do to the house.

The next time she suggested going out I told her that I didn't feel like it as I was to tired and wouldn't enjoy myself. She wasn't very happy, she tried pleading and asking nicely, and when that didn't work told me what a miserable sod I was, how I didn't know how to enjoy myself. It turned into a nasty argument. The one thing I will give her due for is that she wouldn't row in front of my son or anyone else. She said that even if we weren't speaking when we went out as soon as we were in company the row was left behind until we returned home.

She went off that night and asked Christopher to go and play pool with her. I wasn't happy about that, but he was thrilled and I couldn't bear to burst his bubble. I so badly wanted this relationship to work and just then I felt that I was losing her. I didn't really know what to do, so I drove down to the pub later on to pick them up. When I got there Babs said they would just finish their game and I could have a drink while I was waiting for them. She seemed in a good enough mood, but there again she could be saving it until we got home.

I didn't wait to find out. I just got my son off to bed as quickly as I could. I told Babs that I was going up to bed, she seemed all right and said she wouldn't be long.

The next day she said she was going to get a job – on the side of course, where no one knew her. I was instructed to tell anyone who asked that she was visiting relatives. I thought that this was her way of telling me she was moving on, forgetting that the house was in both our names. She just said that she was sick to death of me moaning about money and doing up the house and that she was going to get extra money somehow. *How come I'm always in the wrong?*

Moving on, she got a job cooking for students at a live-in riding school at Harrogate, five days on and two days off. She didn't seem to mind the separation, but I did. She pointed out that we needed the money and she didn't want me working, and how we would be so pleased to see each other at the end of the five days.

Everything went fine for a few weeks. Both Christopher and I spent time at her work, me helping out and Chris learning to ride. He thought that was great. I managed to get the two outhouses plus the kitchen painted, though we were still no further on with carpets or other rooms done. When Babs did come home she only wanted to go out and drink. It got to the point where I was getting very sick of the drinking. One day I was due to take her back after her time off and, while I know shouldn't have done it, I took her house key off the key ring and didn't tell her. In my mind it meant that I could feel safe and secure and not open to debate any more. It didn't work like that at all as she was a joint tenant.

She phoned me that evening and asked why I had taken her key. I told her that I couldn't take any more of the drinking. She cared more for the drink then she did for me and that I wouldn't be picking her up on her days off any more. She said that she would come back under her own steam and we would talk about it properly when she got there.

What could I say? I couldn't tell her I didn't love her any more – I loved her just as much, if not more, than I did when I met her. It was just that I couldn't carry on with her drinking all the time. It wasn't just the money aspect, it altered her personality as well. We hardly ever made love any more, she never said she loved me and if I asked her, she said that it meant nothing as they were only words and could be easily said.

The day that she came home wasn't very good. She just

wanted to sit with her bottle of brandy and drink. She said that she could unwind like that, that was the way she was and, whether I liked it or not, she had half the house and I couldn't put her out. She carried on until I felt like it was all my fault.

The next day she asked me to give her a lift to the town. She said she had some things to do, and that she didn't want to talk with me. She just went off and that was the last I heard of her. However, a week later, Christopher received a letter from her. She had got herself a flat in Darlow, she loved him and maybe she could see him one day in the future. She wrote that she loved his mam as well and he wasn't to blame me for her going.

I felt like I had failed again and swore that I would stay by myself in future. I threw myself into housework, I dug a vegetable patch in the garden and planted it all, but at night after my son had gone to bed... they were the worst. Everything I watched on the TV seemed to remind me of both Babs and Dee. All the music made me cry and I wished that she was here with me instead of in Darlow, I was sure she would soon have someone else as she was so beautiful.

I had in the meantime got myself a little job cleaning the pub across the way, it was only a couple of hours on a morning, but it helped me buy some paint for the house. At least the outhouses and the kitchen were done, but now my heart just wasn't in it. I can remember wishing that I hadn't moved. At least I had known people round there. My new next-door neighbour was OK, but not my kind of person really. She offered herself to me when she found out that Babs had gone. I just couldn't believe it – she had a husband and child. Years later I found out that this sort of thing happened with straight people, they wanted to find out what the other side of the fence was like or else they had tried it before and wanted it again, but with nobody finding out. I, of course, declined. I didn't want to get involved with a married woman, I wasn't one to fool about with anyone else if I had a girlfriend.

I couldn't stand it any more. Babs had written to my son again, so one night after school I asked him if he wanted to go and see her. I guess that I was using him to get to her, but I figured that at least I would find out if she had someone else and if so I could try and get on with my own life again.

When we arrived she had a note stuck on her door saying that she was upstairs, the note was addressed to someone called Shelly. Of course I immediately thought that this was her new women and was just ready to leave when she came running down the stairs and flew into my arms and kissed me. It felt so wonderful. We went into her place and she wanted to take me straight to bed, though of course we couldn't because of Chris. But it didn't matter if we kissed as Babs had explained to my son that when we first got together that when two people loved each other they would want to hug and kiss.

She said that she had hoped that I would come and that she loved me so much; she wanted to work it out and asked if she could come home with me. We were to tell anyone who asked that she had been visiting friends. Of course I couldn't tell her that most people knew she had left me, a part of me was too frightened that she would go again. Even though I knew that I was better off money-wise, and that I could decorate the house sooner if she wasn't there, I didn't want to be by myself. I needed someone to love me and someone who I could love in return. The trouble was, even if someone did love me I still couldn't see why, because when it came down to it, I didn't love myself.

XVII

Babs wanted to keep the flat on in Darlow, she said as a safety net in case I threw her out again. The trouble was I hadn't thrown her out, she had left, but I didn't want to go into that. I was just happy that she was home again.

Things were all right for a couple of weeks then she went off again. She said that she was just going to see if everything was all right at the flat. I of course wanted her to give it up and told her it wasn't fair for her to have somewhere to run off to anytime she wanted. It was a waste of money too for her to be paying rent over when that money could be going into our house.

She said that she would think about it while she was there. She was going to spend the night as she wanted to catch up with the friends that she had made when she lived there. I asked if she was seeing someone else, but she just laughed and said that she didn't want anyone else. She didn't return for two days and when she did come home she was shaking and sweating. She said that she had been taking drugs and they had made her feel good; she wanted me to try it because then I would 'relax and stop worrying'.

If there was one thing I was against, it was any kind of drugs; I told her that and asked that she would never bring them home. She called me old fashioned and said that most lesbians took dope now, it was the 'in' thing. Well not to me it wasn't, I was sticking to what I had first said, after all, look at the state of her.

We spent the night in each other's arms, but not a romantic way. She was still shaking and kept saying she was cold. How I hoped that this would never happen again. She said she had given the flat up and that she was going back to work if I would take her. She promised things would be different this time and we would get the house done up. I wasn't sure that I believed her, but wanted to give it another chance. I just didn't want to end up on my own again.

It lasted about two weekends and then she started complaining that she worked hard all week and had nothing to relax with at the weekend. Finally she announced that if she wanted a drink then she would have one and that was the end of it. She told me straight up that if I didn't like it, well there was nothing I could do as it was half her house. What do they say? *If you can't beat 'em, join 'em.* Don't believe it – I could not drink like her and I wasn't sure if I wanted to.

Babs had promised to buy my son a new bike that weekend and when I reminded her about that she said that he wouldn't mind if she got it another day. I was furious. I knew Christopher had been really looking forward to that and had told all his friends he was getting a new bike. So I went off in the car. I had worked it out so that my money would come on Monday and if I took some out of the bank now, it could be put back next week. I didn't think about anything except his bike, but in the back of my mind I knew that I wasn't going to be around to worry about it.

Christopher was over the moon with his bike and that's all that mattered. It's funny how sometimes you just can't see that what you are about to do will matter to anyone, you're just so desperate to get out of it and figure nobody will miss you as nobody loved you anyway.

I asked my son not to stray too far from the play area in the village and told him that I loved him and that whatever happened he was the best thing that had ever happened to me. Of course he didn't care, he was a child, all he cared about was playing with his friends and riding his new bike – and what child wouldn't?

I went back to the house. By this time Babs was away with the drink. She said that I knew that she was going to get the bike for Christopher, but now that I had gone and been clever and got it instead she just hoped that I could pay for it because she wouldn't now. I told her that I didn't really care one way or the other, he was happy and hadn't been let down and that's all that mattered. She changed slightly and suggested I join her for a drink, and that we could talk tomorrow. That was the last thing I wanted, so I just told her I was going upstairs for a rest. She started calling me a lazy cow and sneered that it was no wonder that Dee had left me, I would drive anyone insane. She told me she hoped that I didn't think she was going to turn her music down as at least she knew how to enjoy herself, not like me.

I guess that was the straw that broke the camel's back. I got a glass of water and went upstairs. I didn't think of anything or anyone, I just knew that I didn't want to live any more. What good was I anyway? I couldn't keep a relationship going, couldn't keep my house, it was just as bad as the day we moved in and it was all my fault.

When I had bought the bike I had also bought a bottle of extra strong painkillers, hoping that it would be the end for me. Some hope – I couldn't even seem to do that right. Babs followed me upstairs and when she saw what I was going to do she said if that's what I wanted she would help me. She forced my mouth open and shoved some pills in. She said that she wasn't going to call for help for anyone so stupid and useless. Then she slapped me and went back down to the drink.

She was so angry. I guess I had pushed her too far. I lay down on the bed for a while trying to make sense of everything. About the only good thing in my life was my son and then I seemed to come to my senses and realise that I was letting him down. I got up and heard Babs talking away to herself or her music, I wasn't sure which. All I did know was that suddenly I had to get away and get my son away too. I was feeling a bit woozy, but felt more sick than anything else. I went and picked up Christopher and his new bike and told him we were going to show his grandmother his new bike. He seemed OK with that.

I had to stop the car a couple of times as I was sick. Stupidly, I didn't realise that all the pills did was make me sick until they were out of my system. Of course I didn't expect any sympathy off my mother, it was more or less an 'I told you so' sort of attitude, but at least she looked after my son.

The next day my younger brother phoned up my home to see if Babs was still there. I really couldn't deal with it as my stomach was too sore and hurt. Anyway to cut a long story short, I had torn the lining in my stomach and only time would put it right.

My brother got no response when he called, so it seemed like there was no one at the house. I wanted to go back but I was pretty scared about going up on my own, so he said he would take me. When we arrived the house was dark and quiet and definitely empty. It looked like she had returned to work, though how she got there I don't know, but at that moment I didn't really care.

I started to think about how I could to get my old house back. The council said that because we had a joint tenancy agreement there was nothing I could do without Babs giving up her tenancy as well – fat chance of that happening.

I had been back at the house a week when Babs phoned. She said that she was sorry and she would be coming home the following weekend and we could discuss where we would go from there. She told me that she still loved me, but I knew I couldn't go through the drinking game again, I told her that she needed some help with the drinking and I would support her if she wanted to get it. She insisted she didn't have a problem, but promised that we would talk about it when she came home. I didn't want to be there when she arrived, but couldn't listen to my mother going on, so I took my son to Peggy's. She had always supported me and been a good friend to me. We had been staying with her for a couple of days when I got a call from social services officer. They had picked up Babs at a roundabout a couple of miles from home and she was now waiting in the town's small hospital. She was drunk as a skunk and all she wanted was me.

I didn't really want to see her as I knew how soft I was, but the social services woman wanted me to go, she seemed to think that it would help. I went. I still loved her, you can't just stop loving someone because of the way they are.

When I arrived at the hospital Babs was sitting in the corner of the room on a chair, she had been crying and looked a wreck. I felt so guilty, immediately I was sure it was all my fault, I was the one who turned my back on the relationship. The doctor wanted her to be admitted into a mental ward in York. She didn't want to as she still didn't think she had a problem. I told her that we couldn't go on as we had been, we didn't even make love any more because of her drinking problem; that, finally, seemed to register with her. I said that I would come every day to see her. She asked me to collect her wages for her and tell them that she wouldn't be returning as she couldn't stand the pressure. I promised I would and said that I would see her the following day.

She seemed to be happy with that and agreed to go into the hospital.

It was hard finding the money to visit. I had her wages as she said to keep them and get her cigs etc. It was about three days later that the social services called on me. I was back in my own home by this time, and they told me that the doctor at the hospital had said that Babs could be very dangerous because of the drinking and that as far as they were concerned my son was at risk. They warned me that if I were to carry on my relationship with Babs there was a possibility that they would take my son away. There was not question as to what I was going to do. My son came first. Nevertheless, it was one of the worst things that I have ever had to do. I felt terrible, she was still in hospital and there I was deserting her just when she needed me most.

The social worker said that she would take me so I wouldn't have the added problem of driving, When we arrived Babs was all happy and pleased to see me, but I couldn't stay. I had to tell her straight away then leave, get it over with. I told her that I couldn't see her any more, I didn't explain why. She said that she wasn't bothered; she had already met someone in the city when she was allowed out. I believed her at the time, but thinking back now I know that it was just a front.

So back to an empty house, well apart from my son who – bless him – wasn't a great deal of company. After his homework he just wanted to go out and play. I reckon about the only good thing that had come out of this move was the fact that the small village school had really brought Christopher out of his shell.

The only thing to do now was to try and get back to my old house in Thirske and the only way to do that was through an exchange as before. But who wants to be in a little village these days? You can but hope.

I started packing boxes, willing something to turn up. I closed up the living room so I could use it for storage and just lived in the kitchen.

It took less time than I expected to find someone who wanted an exchange. I just had to get them to see the house and then see theirs and the ball could start rolling. I kept my fingers crossed that they would want my house. I wasn't bothered about what I got, as long as it was back in Thirsk. They had a top-storey flat which would mean walking down two flights of stairs every time the dog wanted out, but whatever.

The move went through pretty quick. Like the last time we hired a van between us so it didn't cost too much. The next thing for me was to find myself a job. Though I was kind of relieved that I only had myself to please, I did find it very lonely. But I didn't have a lot of time to feel sorry for myself once I had a job, as there was a lot to do in the flat. Also I had sorted out an arrangement with the people in the other flats over the garden which meant that I could fence a piece off for the dog and have a piece of lawn to sit out in come summer. That and the decorating kept me so busy that I didn't have time to think.

The good thing about me moving back into Thirsk was the fact that I had plenty of people I knew to go out with, even if it was only shopping at least it was a chance to be with a grown up person.

One of my friends was a lady called May, she had a son just a week older than Christopher, in fact she was one of the first people to visit me at the maternity hospital. She would come round to my house and I went to her house and the two lads played together. It was nice to have some company when I was not at work. We took the dogs out for walks, or had coffee down in the town when we did the shopping. Four doors away lived my niece and her partner so we would go down there of an evening. Still there was something missing. I needed someone special in my life, someone to love as I had so much love to give. If only May had been gay it would have been great as we got on so well!

May and I were down in town shopping and who should I see, but Dee. My heart skipped a beat, *what was she doing back and seemingly by herself?* I said hello as she didn't seem as if she was going to speak, I only later found out that she thought May was my new girlfriend.

Well I was on cloud nine for the rest of the day, but my mind was going round in circles: *was she back for good? Was she still with the one she ran off with? Did she even think about me?* because I had sure as hell thought about her.

I forgot to mention that I was seeing a girl from Sheffield at that time. It wasn't a serious relationship, in fact as far as I was concerned it wasn't a relationship at all. She read more into it and did things like printing a verse in the local paper for Valentine's Day and giving me her last Rollo with a ring in the box. I guess that it boosted my confidence at the time and I also found it difficult to hurt her so even though I thought of it as more of a friendship I just let it carry on. I had to let her down gently when it came to the bedroom though. The truth was she didn't turn me on at all, but I've never really been able to speak out about anything, and I found I just couldn't tell her how things really were.

Anyway, moving on, I had a job working nine to three so it fitted in with Christopher's schooling. He seemed to be enjoying school just then. When he came home he did his homework and the little jobs that he had to do each evening. I always got him involved in the house because I figured it would stand him in good stead when he eventually started courting and I didn't think that there's one job for the men and that washing up and such things were women's work.

After we had eaten we used to take Scamp his little dog for a walk. Sometimes he would go out with one of his friends and take the dog with him, but he wasn't one for having a lot of friends, he seemed to prefer being on his own with his music or books, or even just walking the dog by himself.

We had a young girl in the flat beneath us – well, I say young, she was in her early twenties. She had a fourteen-month-old toddler and when she didn't have a babysitter he used to come up and stay with us. Christopher was ever so good with him and used to play with him. The baby wasn't a very good talker yet, but his mam seemed to think he'd got better since we had started looking after him.

His mam went out a lot, four or five times a week, and I guess that the fact we didn't ask for any babysitting money made me an easy target for looking after him. I didn't mind though, I didn't go out much and when I did it wasn't in my home town. In any case, I really liked children. I once asked Chris if he would have liked some brothers or sisters, but he said he wouldn't as then he would have to share his things and he didn't want that.

I still kept thinking about Dee and looking out for her if I went down the town. Two weeks went by and I still hadn't seen her again, so I began to think that she had only been home for a visit and was still with the woman she went off with. Then, one Monday, I was in town and heard someone calling my name. It was Dee. She asked me if I wanted to go for a cup of coffee with her – is the sky blue? I didn't want to seem too eager because I didn't know if she was on her own again or not, and besides, she was the one who had nearly sent me round the bend when she left me and I didn't want to go through it all again.

I told her that I would meet her in about half an hour after I had done the shopping. Truth be told all I wanted to do was forget the shopping and go with her straight away. As soon as I saw her I knew that I still loved her and whatever she'd done, it no longer mattered. She had been my first proper lover and I hoped she would be my last. So an hour later we met for coffee and talked. She said that she was by herself now, she gave no explanation as to why and I didn't probe. She asked if that lady she had seen me with twice was my new girlfriend and that just tickled me pink. She had met May long ago, back when we were together, but she had clearly forgotten.

I told her that there was no one in my life right now, which was quite true as I didn't consider the women from Sheffield to be a girlfriend so she never even crossed my mind. We were both very wary of starting something up again, but I still suggested that she should drop in for a coffee if she ever happened to be in my area. She was surprised I had a new address, though she understood that I had to move on, that there were too many memories in the old house. She just said that it was a shame, after all, we had done up the house that we had shared together.

It didn't take her long to drop round: she was on my doorstep the next night and it wasn't because she was in the area. She said that she just wanted to see me again and that she still loved me and hadn't really stopped loving me. Like a fool I believed it all. I so badly wanted it to be true.

Thinking about it, why hadn't she come back before now? She said that she had been landed with her girlfriend's two children when she ran off with her boyfriend. Dee had been left to settle the debts left and get the social services in to do something about the children. She asked me about Babs and what happened there. I simply said that it was in the past and I wanted to forget about it now.

Christopher actually seemed pleased to see her and they talked to one another OK. I was babysitting the little boy from the flat below us that night and Dee said would I mind if she stopped and helped out. Did I mind? That was a laugh. We spent a lovely evening together, we played some music and did a lot of talking. I confessed that I still loved her and was sorry for the way things had turned out with us. I told her how I had tried to do things right with Babs as I thought I hadn't done right with her but that it still hadn't worked out.

She said that and she thought about me also and asked if there was there a chance of us trying again. I said I thought I would like that. After that we kissed and things got a bit heavy. I found it very hard to stop her touching me, I wanted her as much as she wanted me, but knowing that the woman she had gone off with had been around a bit I couldn't sleep with her until she had been checked out. She understood, which I was surprised at, she didn't like doctors at all. She said that she would get a job and get checked and anything else that I wanted her to do. I told her to do it for herself not for me.

We spent most nights together till she got a job and she then moved in. I saw the results from the doctor and everything was OK. It was wonderful to lay in her arms again after making love and I will always say she was a most considerate lover, she always pleased me first before thinking of herself. You see, she could only ever have one orgasm whereas I could go on and have several.

XVIII

It was nice having her back to love and be loved. On the weekends we did the housework together and I baked, both she and Christopher loved their food. Sometimes we would go out for a drink, but mainly we stayed at home. We didn't need anyone else at that time. I still had the car and we would often go up to Redcar where Dee like to play on the slot machines. Chris and I would walk along the beach with the dog and then we'd all meet up later for something to eat.

It became a bit of a problem getting Dee off the machines; it would often lead to a row as she thought that I was nagging her. I never had a lot of money to play the machines and would get annoyed that she was wasting money.

The problem was although we lived together all Dee gave me was 'lodge money'. She had a good, and sometimes greedy, want for food – she would think nothing of eating a big tub of ice cream to herself and – while it would give me great pleasure to cook good meals – for her it wasn't cheap.

One weekend Dee had to work overtime. She didn't mind working, she always was a good worker, but she seemed to live for her work more than anything else. It could have just been me being possessive. I wanted to be with her every minute of the day and night. Christopher and I took our dog Scamp out through the fields then we drove down in the car and then took him swimming. Christopher went into the water with Scamp. It was a nice day, Christopher was going to go to the pictures with his latest friend so it meant that Dee and I had the evening to ourselves. I thought I would cook her a nice meal, get in a bottle of wine and dress up for her. She liked it when I wore skirts and makeup. I really didn't feel comfy dressed up, but it was a small price to pay to make her happy.

Anyway, so we arrived home, Christopher went running upstairs with Scamp and I had to pop to the local shop. I started reversing the car, there was a clear space to get into, nothing in the way, or so I thought. I didn't see Scamp, I thought he was upstairs with my son, but he had ran out when he heard the car. I ran right over him, killing him outright. I was devastated, and so was my son. It was good job that Dee was due home because I couldn't let go of him. I felt like a murderer. If anyone had asked me for the car that day I would have given it to them.

Dee took charge, she never seemed to be affected by death or anything that dealt with emotions; though I was grateful for her dealing with things like Scamp's death, I did believe deep down that she didn't have deep feelings. She said that she hadn't had a very good childhood as her mother used to force her to do things she didn't want to do or make her read knowing it was difficult for her, which was why she couldn't write a letter properly or never read. All that sort of thing were left to me, so I suppose in one sense it worked out OK, but it would have been nice to see some emotion as she never cried over anything.

I lasted two days without an animal, but the house seemed so empty; I went to the nearest animal shelter and choose a puppy to give to my son when he came in from school. She was ever so cute, a little bundle of fluff. She was a cross between a collie and a German shepherd so she was going to be a fair size when she grew up. I decided to leave the naming to Christopher when he came in. I hoped he would like her and she him as much as Scamp had, but I never gave a thought to what Dee would think. I guess that was part of the problem thinking back: I never considered her thought on things around the house or I'd just go ahead and make decisions that would affect all of us. Maybe if she hadn't thought of herself as a lodger but rather as an equal partner, things would have been better, who knows.

Christopher didn't seem to be all that thrilled about the puppy, he sat with her a while then said he had to do his homework. Maybe it was too soon after Scamp for him to have another puppy. I couldn't tell, he could be a strange child, he wouldn't talk to me about things, but keep it all inside him. It would come out when we had words over something and then he would throw the problem up. I don't know where I went wrong on that front, as I always told him that I loved him and he always came first in everything. I never wanted him to feel the way I did when I was a child.

Unfortunately this caused problems between Dee and I. She always griped about how my darling son could do no wrong, but that was untrue. I knew he was no saint, but he did come first. He was my number one and she knew that. I told her it wasn't a contest between them I loved them both, but with a different kind of love for each of them. Sometimes it wasn't easy.

We were still looking after the little boy from downstairs, in fact his mother had just told me that she was pregnant and the father was the latest chap she was going out with. She said he knew about it and he would stay with her. I got the knitting needles out and started making baby things. I didn't quite know how Dee felt about it. She got on well with the little boy and would say that it would have been nice if we could have had another child and we often talked about it, but I didn't feel like I could go through all that again. I said that it would be down to her as she was younger and fitter then me, but she said that she was still a virgin and that's how she was going to stay. Her sister, who had just moved in across the street, told me that Dee wasn't a virgin at all because a virgin was someone without any sexual experience. What did it matter, I asked myself, but I could tell it mattered to Dee. She said that I should have defended her, but I couldn't when I felt that she wasn't right. That caused her to have one of her sulks and refuse to speak to me. It all ended up in a row as the silence drove me round the bend. Why she couldn't talk about things as normal people did, I don't know.

Time passed and we added another dog to our family. My son didn't take to the first one, Sandie, and as Dee's sister's dogs had produced a litter I choose one for Christopher. It was cross between a shepherd and a Munsterlander and he was a big lad when he grew up. The other reason for me getting another dog was because Sandie, bless her, was very destructive. I had heard about a dog trainer who worked locally, in fact the person who told me about the trainer said that she had heard they were gay as it was two women who ran the company, and if I'm honest that was the main reason why I went down to see them. I thought that Dee and I might have some gay friends around us; it would have been nice, but it wasn't to be. There were two women, but also a chap. In any case, one of them told me to either get a cage or a friend for Sandie. She said that it might work or I could get double trouble with two of them! I couldn't imagine keeping her in a cage, it seemed cruel to me to pen an animal up.

The trainer had two dogs herself and they were very well-trained. They were both border collies and they could do tricks and play dead all sorts. She was a very friendly person and said that if I wanted to go down and watch one Thursday evening I would be very welcome. I thought that sounded great. I never thought about asking if Dee could come and hoped that it wouldn't cause a row between us, but she seemed to be quite happy for me to go. She said that she would do some work around the place that she couldn't when I was around as I always wanted to know where she was and what she was doing. She had a point. I always wanted her to be with me.

Christopher didn't seem very happy to be left with Dee. I couldn't see the problem myself as she always seemed to be getting on OK with him when I was around. I remember someone once saying that your kids end up growing up and leaving you so that they can do their own thing. When they do leave they don't care if you are by yourself or not, so you should live your life for yourself and to hell with anyone else.

Of course, my problem has been that I always listened to everyone else's advice but I didn't have a mind to follow it. I could never say no to anything anyone asked me to do for them. Dee, on the other hand, thought it was easy to say no to anyone if she didn't want to do whatever they asked of her. That was a major difference between us, I was soft and I thought she was too hard.

Anyway, I started going along to the dog classes with Sandie; I found it really good and my dog enjoyed it. I had also made a new friend. It turned out that I knew the chap who lived there very well as I worked for him when I was pregnant with my son. He was a nice guy. I couldn't work out what the relationship was between him and the two women, but Sandra, the dog trainer, soon told me that he was a partner in business with the other lady. Sandra didn't have a good word for this other woman. She was always all right with me, but then I didn't have to live with any of them.

My life was very busy at this time as the girl downstairs had a baby girl, Nicola, and the father had of course left. She managed to stay in for the first week and then asked me if I would look after the baby as well as her boy. Dee said that she was taking me for a ride, but I didn't really mind as I loved children. I would have had more if I hadn't been gay or things had been different.

I went to the dog training once a week and went for nice long walks with the two dogs; I ran the house and worked at a chip shop of an evening as well as looking after the two children from downstairs. I needed the money as Dee never paid any bills or anything as regards the house. I remember one time I had a large gas bill and she said that she would lend me the money to pay it and she would take it off her lodge each week until it was paid back. Lend it? Funny kind of a relationship if you ask me, I always thought you should throw all the money in together and pay bills and buy food like that, but she still maintained that she was a lodger. It did cause a few arguments I must say, but she wouldn't change.

It seemed to be that we had the baby more often than the mother did. The mother brought her cot to keep upstairs when she was sleeping with us. The mother had got a job and as I was always fetching the baby up. I asked the mother to give me some authority in case the child was ill or anything like that, so she had a letter drawn up by a solicitor.

Just as well that she did, as it wasn't long after that Nicola had to be taken into hospital. I was ever so worried, she couldn't keep anything down because she was coughing so much. She was diagnosed as an asthmatic. Dee had to go round the pubs to find the mother because the hospital needed to see her personally to tell her about it as the letter she gave me wasn't good enough. She visited Nicola a couple of times and then said that she knew she was OK with me and left it at that. We didn't see so much of the little boy any more as his grandmother wanted him. She said that he was her favourite, but she never really bothered about Nicola, it was as if she didn't exist.

I had suffered with back problems after the birth of my son and had seen the doctor on numerous occasions to get tablets of one sort or another for the pain. It used to ache and act up every now and then, and now I was having a few problems with my back again and had to visit the hospital twice a week for treatment. I took Nicola with me, though it was rather awkward lifting the pram up and down from the flat. I decide to see the council to find out if we could get a house on medical grounds and also on the grounds that I had Nicola. I asked her mother if it was OK to say that I had a baby to look after and she was fine about that.

It wasn't too long before they gave us a three-bedroom house just more or less round the corner from the flat. Dee said that we wouldn't have to get a removal van as most things could be carried round and she got her sister's husband to give her a hand. I thought that now that we weren't just upstairs Nicola's mam would want Nicola back, but she told us to take the cot and everything with us for now.

Before long Nicola was a year old and calling me 'mam'; her own mother knew and just laughed about it. Of course I actually felt like her mother as I was bringing her up. I could count the times she had been home on one hand.

Life was looking pretty good just then. Dee had just asked me to marry her, she said that then she would feel more secure that it was her house as well as mine, funny girl. I was thrilled. Of course it wouldn't be recognised as a legal marriage, but would make us very happy. It wasn't difficult to find a vicar who would perform the ceremony, we found one through *The Gay News*. He said that he didn't want anything for doing the 'blessing' so long as we could just pay for the petrol he used coming to us. We fixed a date, bought the rings and got a good friend to make a cake and look after the catering. My mother didn't want to know, she said that we would be a laughing stock in the town and she wanted nothing to do with us. Dee didn't even to bother telling her mother as she would have probably said the same thing.

However, my sister and Dee's sister and May acted as our witnesses and a few close friends came too. We held the whole thing at our house. Dee wanted Nicola to go back to her mother's for the day so we wouldn't have to worry about a baby, but her mam said that she would be OK with us as she was busy. Dee didn't like that at all.

By the time the vicar came to give us the blessing Dee was pretty well gone. She hit the vodka bottle as soon as the guests and friends started coming round, as she said that she was a bag of nerves. Later on she said that she couldn't even remember the ceremony at all.

When everyone was eating and drinking Dee disappeared. Her sister went to look for her and found her in Nicola's room crying. She said that I didn't care about her, I only cared about Nicola and my darling son. Well that was just nonsense. Of course I cared about her, but it was no good trying to talk to her as she was quite drunk at this time.

Her sister and I decided the best thing to do was to put her to bed, though it didn't look very good as we had just taken vows. The last thing I wanted was for people to know that we were having a domestic, so I told them that she was very drunk, owing to having downed a bottle of vodka to soothe her nerves, and that we had put her to bed.

People stayed for about an hour after that and then started leaving. Nicola had been ever so good, but then again she always was. Christopher helped me to tidy up and get Nicola ready for bed. She loved him like a big brother and he was ever so good with her. While most thirteen-year-olds would want to be out and about with their friends, Christopher was a homebird.

Things didn't change, only the fact that we both wore rings. Dee was still very moody and wouldn't talk anything over. She would just stay quiet and that really got to me. I would end up losing it and saying a lot of things that I didn't mean, like calling her immature and saying she was mean with money. It would usually end up with a horrible silence for about two days than she would come home with some flowers or chocolates and apologise. I couldn't get it through to her that it would all be so much easier to talk things over in the first place.

There were times when she would pack her bags and go and get herself a bed-sit in the town, or pack up and move a few miles away. She couldn't see how much this hurt me as she thought that it had been me who drove her to it. She took it all as a case of 'who was the boss'. She wanted to make all the decisions and didn't understand that no one should be the boss in any relationship, but that you should talk things over. I was left to make most of the decisions as I ran the household and took care of everyone paid the bills. I said that she could have all the money and run things if she wanted to do so, but she said that as she was at work all the time and I didn't work she hadn't time really. I felt that I couldn't win. It hurt at first that she kept going off, but after a while I got used to it.

One night after she had just returned from one of her walkabouts, as I called them, she talked about us going on holiday with Nicola and Christopher. I said it was a lovely idea, but pointed out that I never had any spare money for holidays, so she said that she would pay for it and save all the spending money also. I hadn't had a holiday for six years and I was couldn't wait to get away. We booked a caravan at Skegness. There was plenty on the site for the kids to do and a babysitting service so we could go out if we wanted to do so. The kids loved it and we never had a cross word between us. We never even used the babysitting service. We were quite happy to stay in when the little ones went to bed, or sometimes Dee would go out with Christopher while I stayed in. They would go and play pool at the club, she would have a few beers and he would have soft drinks. They seemed to be getting on pretty well at that time. She said that I could go out if I wanted and she would sit in, but I never really wanted to. We had to make sure that Christopher was well asleep before we went to bed though, as I was a very noisy person when we made love.

All too soon the holiday came to an end and it was back to reality; the dogs were happy to see us back. We had left them with Sandra the dog trainer, as she ran boarding kennels as well as the dog school. Dee didn't really like her, she said that Sandra fancied me. I thought that was rot, she was going out with the chap who owned the place, although it was a bit weird that when she sent Christmas cards to me, she never put Dee's name on.

Anyway, whatever the rumours, she ended up marrying the chap who owned the place, or rather joint-owned it. Sandra was not very happy about the arrangement, she wanted to get rid of Vera, the other owner. She tried her best to make life uncomfortable for her like turning off the TV when a certain soap was on and nagging about her going in and out without changing her shoes or removing them. She would cook a meal for herself and her husband and leave Vera out. She said that if Vera wanted something, she could fix it herself as she wasn't catering for anyone. It made it a bit difficult when I went down to see her as I had nothing against Vera. She came up to my house one night and said that she was thinking of moving because Sandra was being so horrible. She said that they would have to buy her out and she didn't think they would be able to do that,

To cut a long story short, Sandra and her husband got someone to undervalue the property and they told Vera that they would pay her money every month until she was paid the sum that they said she was entitled. She was just pleased to get out of there, so she accepted their deal. She had a small caravan and told me that she would be living in that until she could arrange something else. She would camp in the lay-by where the gypsies were. I didn't tell Sandra that she had talked to me, I know she wouldn't approve and she had a way of making you feel uncomfortable or wrong for disagreeing with her, so it was easier to keep it to myself.

Vera did come up to us for a bath and we visited her one night as we both felt sorry for her as she had a rough deal. Dee was more against Sandra than before, but as I wanted to train my dog I still went down there. We would sometimes go down during the day as it was a nice walk for my dogs and Nicola liked going out for a walk. It was a bit awkward sometimes with the buggy, but I wouldn't have it any other way, Nicola seemed more like a daughter than a foster child. She certainly kept me going as well; if I did have a bad day with my back then I would rest when she did. Dee was very good with everything when I wasn't well. She would take over when she came in from work and prepare things for the next day. She would get annoyed that Nicola's mother wasn't taking her home, but I said just to leave it as it was. Nicola was a very good baby anyway.

I still had to go for physiotherapy twice a week, but I would leave Nicola's pram in the car and she would usually go to sleep when we got to the hospital. Her real mother knew that I had to go twice a week, but never said that she would take her home. It would have interfered with her going out with whoever she wanted to both during the day and of a night. Gary, her little boy, would go to his grandma's most times, but there was the odd times that he came to me.

He was at school then, so it was only a case of meeting him except for a weekend, but he would trail around after Dee whatever she was doing and Christopher would take him in his room and play cars or something with him. I bought them toys as they were always with us so we didn't have to trail them back and forth. Dee got a bit petty sometimes, but I would tell her it wasn't her money going on the toys or anything else for the kids, their mother gave me her family allowance money for Nicola. She kept the social security money for her, but to tell the truth it wasn't about money as far as I was concerned. I just loved them, how could you not?

I supposed one day her mother would want her back for good, but there was no sign of it yet. I signed her up for a toddlers group and she loved it. We went twice a week; there were times when a teacher had to take over if it got to energetic, but on the whole I loved it as much as Nicola did.

We would also go swimming of an evening as Dee enjoyed that. She would take Nicola in, of course, as I still didn't like the water. Christopher had made a new friend and it was good for him to be with someone his own age instead of with me and the kids, but I did miss him being around the place. Still it wouldn't be long before he left school. Where did the years go? He didn't know what he wanted to do for a living, but no doubt he would when the time came.

It was summer now and Dee spent most of her time after work on the garden as it was a real mess. I know it's pretty juvenile, but I always felt left out when she wasn't with me. I sometimes thought that she would rather be outside or anywhere than be with me. With my insecurities I never could understand how anyone could love me or what they saw in me, I still feel like that even today, though better than how I used to be. Dee and I had our ups and downs, more downs then ups it seemed, but it was great making up.

We decided that seeing as we had Nicola most of the time, and her brother some of the time, we would make the spare room into their room. We bought bunk beds, or rather I did, out of a catalogue and bought a football quilt for Gary and a fairy one for Nicola. We kitted the room out with kids wallpaper, and we put a bookshelf in so that I could read stories to them at bedtime. I suppose I had more fun with them than I did with my own son as I had more time and only worked of an evening, unlike when I brought him up and had to work all the time. I felt bad about that, but he seemed to be a normal happy lad, so I must have done something right.

Nicola was about two and a half now and a worker from Social Services called on a regular basis. They said that it was just routine as they could see that she was a happy, well-adjusted little girl, but that they were there if I ever had any problems. I didn't know at that time what a big problem was around the corner.

Nicola's mother was courting a soldier named Christopher, one of the many that passed through at that, and they had Nicola on the odd weekend. I guess he was trying to prove that he accepted her children, but Nicola seemed quite happy to go. The odd time Tracy would end up fetching her back to me, claiming that Nicola wasn't well and had asked for me, though she always seemed OK when she returned and not ill at all.

One Sunday evening when she had returned I was bathing her and she said that her winky hurt – she called her private part that name as that's what I had taught her. I said that if it still hurt tomorrow I would take her to the doctors, thinking that she maybe had an infection. Then she said that Christopher had hurt her winky. I told her that it would be all right as I loved her and would look after her. I then asked Dee what she thought. She didn't know what to say or do, so I decided that I would phone the social services and take it from there.

The social worker said to make sure that she didn't go to her mother's house, but to make up some excuse if her mother or boyfriend asked to take her and that they would be round first thing in the morning. I settled her down for the night and wondered what Social services would do. I couldn't believe that someone could hurt her like that, she was only a little girl. At least when it happened to me I was grown up to a certain extent. I had so many feelings going round in my head, anger being the main one. Dee said to wait until we had seen the social worker and take it from there. It was awful when they came, no one could ask a direct question as we could be blamed for prompting her, so it all had to come out naturally and of course she seemed to have forgotten about it. As far as she was concerned she was home now and happy and secure where no one could hurt her.

The social worker said that we would have to take her to Northallerton Hospital to be examined. Dee didn't go to work that day as she wanted to be there for me and Nicola, which I really appreciated. We took her to the hospital and met the social worker there. The doctor confirmed that she had been interfered with, not full-blown sex, but that someone had definitely been touching her. I felt gutted, how could anyone touch a little girl like that? The social worker said that they would have to inform her mother, but that I had to keep her and was not to let her mother take her. She said that they would have to have a meeting to see where they went from here.

I tried to carry on as normal, but found it difficult knowing that the man who had done this was just around the corner. But things had to be normal for Nicola's sake. The social worker came round next day and said that Nicola was safe and secure where she was with me, so they were going to leave her as she was. Thank God for that, I wouldn't have been able to stand it if I lost her. They also asked us to go to a children's unit at the hospital where hopefully they would get Nicola to talk about what had happened to her and the police would take a video to analyse. It was like any ordinary room, full of toys; a plain-clothed policewoman was in the room with her and we were given the option to sit in another room and watch what was going on. But Nicola just played with toys and they couldn't get her to tell them anything.

I felt like I was living on the edge of a volcano ready to erupt at any second, not knowing what was going to happen, if I would lose my little girl. I couldn't see her mother letting me keep her after all this. It was because of me that her boyfriend was being questioned.

I had a week's grace before the social workers had another

meeting and I spent every minute that I could with Nicola. How I loved her. I know that she had been born to someone else, but she had been with me pretty much since the day she was born. I had fed her and clothed her, but most of all loved her, I couldn't bear the thought of losing her.

The head of social services along with the normal social worker arrived one Friday evening and said that Nicola's mother had accused my son, Christopher, of touching her daughter and that she hadn't known that I was a lesbian. She thought that Dee was just a friend who lodged with me and if she had known about the relationship she would not have left her child with us. She also said that every time she wanted her daughter home we had some reason to keep Nicola from being at home with her, her mother.

Isn't it wonderful how people can come up with things that aren't true when they are at fault? She never wanted Nicola from the day she was born, but she drew the money for her that would pay for her nights out.

They said that under the circumstances they had found a foster home for Nicola and had to take her that evening. They asked me to I pack some things for her ready to go. I couldn't get upset then, for Nicola's sake I told her she was going on holiday and that Mammy (me) couldn't come, but there would be some other children and a nice lady and man there to look after her and that I would see her soon. She was a bright little girl and accepted that, but how I kept from breaking down when she wrapped her little arms round my neck and gave me a big kiss I will never know. As I waved her goodbye I broke down. Why me? Why this? She was happy here and now she was going off to god knows who or what. They wouldn't understand all her ways and it's not like her mother could tell them, she didn't know her daughter. It was like a bereavement. I sobbed my heart out. To make matters worse, they had taken my son for questioning.

I begged him, cursed him, asked him how he could do such a thing to me or to Nicola; he swore he never did anything to her and asked how I could ever think such a thing of him. If I had been thinking straight I never would have even asked him. I knew really that it hadn't been him.

Dee and I had talked about it endlessly. Then Dee remembered something: Nicola never called my son by his full name, she never had done as she found it hard to get her tongue round it when she was little so she called him 'Kiss'. We had just left him with that nickname, figuring that she would learn to say his name properly as she grew older, besides we all sort of thought it was cute. Because she was older when her mother's boyfriend came on the scene, she was able to call him Christopher. It was that that helped me sort out in my head who had touched her.

I think I began to push Dee away at this time; I didn't feel she was really there for me. Yes, she was in one way, coming to the hospital and talking everything over, but when I sobbed my heart out she didn't know how I felt. She couldn't understand the love I felt for the children as she had never been a mother; she was just jealous of them. She wanted to make love as normal and go to Redcar as normal; she said that life carried on. I knew that, but it hadn't even been a week since my world had fallen apart. I would see Nicola on every bus ride I took and every place I looked. All I wanted was Christopher back; even though he had grown up he was still my other baby.

After I had made several phone calls, the social worker said that I could see Nicola. It would be at a children's home as I wasn't allowed to know where her foster home was. We arranged a date for the following weekend. I asked if she was OK and she told me that she had settled fine. It wasn't until later that I found out I had been lied to and that Nicola had done nothing except cry for me since they took her away. The day I found out was the day I lost all faith in social workers.

It was so lovely to see her. She ran into my arms. If only I could have taken her back with me, but instead we played with the toys the social worker had left for us, which was something. Dee and I took her for a walk outside; we were only out there a few minutes when the social worker came running out after us. She told us that she thought we had ran off with her, and that she could understand it if we did. She would run away if it had been one of her children, she said. But we couldn't run. For one thing there was nowhere to go, for another it wouldn't have solved anything. The time spent with her went really quickly and she had to be returned to her foster home. The social worker said that she would be in touch soon and we could have another visit the following week. At least I had been allowed to see her, though it wasn't enough. We gave her a cuddle and left. I looked back as I walked down the path and saw she was at the window, waving her little arm goodbye. I wondered if she was as sad as I was, and hoped not.

I was living from one week to the next on the thought that maybe they would fetch her back to me. Her mother was still going out with her Chris and the police didn't seem to be getting anywhere. I didn't think that they would return her while he was still there.

We had a couple more visits and the social workers had one more meeting. To my horror they decided that Nicola's mother would have to get to know her daughter and while we were on the scene she couldn't form a proper bond with her real mother so it was best if we didn't see her any more. How could they do that? They always thought she was OK and happy when she was with me, now everything had changed.

XIX

I ended up on antidepressant tablets, I felt like I was losing my mind, everywhere I went I saw Nicola. I would just sit in her room and cry. Of course, Dee left me again, funny how when things got bad she would cut out. I thought that she had loved Nicola as much as I did, but then, if you remember, I never thought she was capable of deep love for anything or anyone. And she proved that in many ways over the years.

She wrote to me after about a week asking how I was and saying how much she loved me. Yet how could she love me? If she did she would have stayed with me in my time of need. But then again I had shut her out – maybe it was my fault, things always seemed to be my fault.

I asked her to come home, and she said that she would come back at the weekend and we could talk about things. I didn't think that was fair, but agreed with her, as I did love her through thick and thin. That was what it was all about, you stuck by your partner whatever happened.

Well, time marched on and nothing I said or did could fetch my little girl back to me. The social services gave her back to her mother and I later found out that her brother interfered with her as well. What chance did she have? It seemed to me, none at all.

The years rolled by and things carried on. Dee kept leaving and coming back when things got tough; it seemed to be a pattern. She was never really happy even though we had married. She wanted full control, but my mother was still the controller. That much hadn't changed.

I only worked part time of an evening now, even after Nicola had been taken away. The days were very long without her in my life and I swore from that day on I would never get attached to another small child again as the pain of separation was unbearable. Dee seemed to think it was all over with and I should get on with my life and forget that I had had Nicola in my life at all. She seemed to be able to do that, but I would never forget Nicola as long as I lived.

I spent all my afternoons walking with the dogs. They just loved me with no motives in their minds and I put all my love back into them. I had three dogs now as Dee's sister had a litter accidentally, not that there is such a thing as 'accidental' mating where dogs are concerned! He was a large dog crossed with a shepherd and Munsterlander, but had a lovely nature. Though I say I had three dogs, only one of them really belonged to me as one was Christopher's and the other one supposedly belonged to Denise. He was a little terrier and he was very cute.

We, the three dogs and me, would usually end up going by Sandra's during our walks, as she was usually around and would invite me in for coffee. She ended up being a friend, or so I thought. She would then join us with her dogs – two lovely, well-trained collies. We would sometime end up in the club and she would do some training with Sandie; I bet she thought that I was thick as there was so much to take in and she gave me far too much to learn all at once. Still it was good of her to bother at all. Sandie would much rather be playing with Buster, my son's dog.

On one occasion that I remember, Sandie and Buster took off over the fields after rabbits. I got all worked up as they wouldn't listen to me when I called them, they just put their heads down and carried on. Sandra said they had no respect for me and that was why they didn't respond when I called. I guess she was right, but it upset me. I poured all the love that I had into my dogs and I really thought that they loved me as much as I loved them. They did really, it's just that they were dogs and doing what came naturally. At least they never tried to change me in any way unlike Dee.

Dee wanted me to be a 'lady', she wanted me to wear make-up and dress in skirts. I did so to please her, but I always felt like a fish out of water. I preferred my trousers and shirts, in fact I sometimes felt I would have felt better being a guy as there was nothing really femme about me. To this day I still worry if I go out; it's OK in the gay clubs as you can be yourself, but if I go out with straight people I secretly wonder if they are embarrassed by the way I dress. It's so bloody awkward!

Sandra and her husband had a caravan at the back of their bungalow, which they let out as a holiday van to other dog owners. They would fetch their animals and Sandra would give them training and throw in the cost of kenneling, so it was a bargain holiday. At times she would be very busy with it, too. By this time we were very friendly and I would look after the kennels and the place while they went to cat and dog shows. Gary, her husband, didn't like it very much as Sandra couldn't drive, but he didn't have much choice as she wore the pants in that house.

It was through looking after the place that I met a number of interesting people who came on their holidays. One couple were called Pauline and Steve, they had three dogs – two rescues and one Border collie called Hanna. Hanna was related to Sandra's two, she was not as well trained, but a very sweet dog all the same. Sandra said that Pauline and Steve were very well-off and had two nice cars and a lovely home. I didn't worry about material things as they were only that – *material*. They never made me feel out of it in any way.

Pauline, Steve, Dee and I all became good friends. They got two more Border collie puppies and invited Sandra and us down to see the puppies at their house. All Sandra went on about going down there was what a lovely house they had, and by the time we got there I was a nervous wreck. I had no need to be, they were both so welcoming and the puppies were lovely. Pauline said that she didn't know why I didn't get one as I liked them so much. Actually, the real reason was that Sandra always put me off. She said that you had to give such a lot to Border collies as they turned nasty if you didn't; she was right in one sense as they had to have something to do otherwise they would get bored.

To cut a long story short, I got a puppy and did I love her! She was so clever, as bright as a button; she gave me confidence and I was soon taking her to obedience classes up in York, which in turn gave me a new lot of friends. I soon entered classes with my little girl and she soon worked me through beginners. I didn't like the way it was so important for people to win; it seemed that their dog was only any good if it was winning, but that just was not for me I'm afraid.

It was around this time that we found out that Mother had cancer and was given six months to live. My sister came back from America to be with Mother. It was like we were children again. She was so controlling that both of us had to stay at her place and sleep on the floor. My sister said that Mother hadn't been told about the fact she was dying. I used to go outside and hit the wall, have a cry and then come back in as if everything was OK. As usual I tried to tell myself that it wasn't happening and it didn't sink in until I had to go to the doctors and get a certificate which said that she only had six months to live – the point of the certificate being that she could get extra money from the council to make the last months of her life a little easier. When I got it in black and white, I broke down right there in the car and sobbed out my heart. You might say it was stupid after all she'd done to me over the years, but I loved her beyond reason, and now I was scared I'd never know if she loved me or not.

My father was beside himself and didn't know what he was going to do without her. After all the times he'd beaten her you wouldn't have thought that he cared, and yet one night he sat up with us and confessed he was frightened he might hurt her turning over in bed or kick her in his sleep. Why bother now, I asked myself, he kicked her plenty when she was OK. I spent the entire period running back and forth between Mother's house and my own with very little sleep. Dari, my sister, had the latest addition to her family with her, a sweet eighteen-month-old baby girl, but it wasn't really the place to have a child. On the occasions she did take her over, Mother would say she couldn't cope with a small child right then as much as she loved her, she was in too much pain. I still think she should have been told what was going on. Though someone told me much later that she would have known, I was never really comfortable that no one gave her the dignity of telling her that she was dying.

I would go out and buy her special things to eat and read, though for the most part she just seemed to sit in her chair and dozed on and off. Dari wouldn't let anyone in to see her; Mother's best friend Jean called several times and Dari would always say that she was asleep. It's sad really, I have spoken to Jean many times since and she was upset that she was never allowed to see Mother.

Dee was very good at the time, I remember she saw to the animals and looked after the home while I was away. I found it all very stressful as Dari was so bossy, you would think that it was only her mother. Father wanted Dari all the time, which made me wonder if there had been ever anything between them, if he had tried it on with her, if she had given him what he wanted. It's a horrible thought I know, but he always let her do anything she wanted and gave her everything she asked. I guess I will never know the answer to that one.

I haven't said where the rest of the family were. Well, the youngest was round at the old family home, which he had been able to buy. He often came round of an evening after work. His wife wasn't there any more as he had kicked her and the child out after getting a new girlfriend. That ought to give you some idea of what he was like. It turned out to be an ongoing thing in his life, he would always have someone else lined up before he turned the old one out, so to speak.

Edward came through from where he lived with his latest boyfriend. I say latest, as he went through men like they were going out of fashion. David, the eldest, was on holiday with his girlfriend at the time and, although he was informed, he didn't think it was worth it to cut his holiday short. What a bloody family! No wonder my mind was all over the place.

In the evening Dari and our two brothers, Eddie and Mike, would settle down to several cans of beer. They said it relaxed them, but of course when drink was in, sense went out of the window, so I was left to try to get them to keep the noise under control. One night I had had enough and went home for the night. It was pretty good to get a good night's sleep, although I knew that I would have to face Dari the next morning. I wasn't looking forward to that at all, it wasn't that I was frightened of her, rather I just couldn't be doing with the agro.

She said that I had let her down as the child had had a bad night and she had to cope with her as well as our parents. *Well tough*, I thought, though I never did say anything. The last thing my mother needed was fighting in the place so I kept the peace as usual. That night Father was very restless and couldn't settle. He said he had a pain in his chest; as he was awaiting a heart bypass we said that we would call the doctor out, but he wouldn't have that and said that if we did he would walk out. I couldn't use the phone in the house anyway, so, without telling Father, I went down the street and phoned the doctor from a call box.

The doctor came out and more or less said that there was nothing wrong with him. After he had gone we got a racket for calling, Father said that the doctor was nothing but a twat anyway and that we were never to call him again.

Two hours later my father was dead. He went to the bathroom and called out for Dari as I was getting Mother up and settling her in her chair. When Dari went in she found Father on the bathroom floor and I ran to phone the ambulance. Mother didn't seem to know what was going on, which was maybe just as well. Father was dead when they took him away. Mother didn't seem to take it in when we told her, or if she did she wasn't upset or anything. Of course Dari took full control of making the arrangements. I remember one time when the doctor was there seeing Mother, the vicar arrived about Father. Dari pushed past me and said she would see to it. Well you can't be in two places at once. Fortunately, the vicar wasn't put off seeing Mother and speaking there, though Dari wasn't very happy about it. He wanted a bit of history as regards my father's funeral, like where he came from and how they had met – I could have told him a few things. The funeral day soon arrived and Mother seemed OK about it, not the sobbing widow at all.

The church was packed, probably due to the fact that my father had spent years looking after the church yard, cutting the grass and things; after my brother killed himself, he spent every hour down there. If only people knew what a pig he was at home, how much we all suffered.

Everyone thought he was a lovely man and he had a write up in the parish magazine praising him and saying how much he would be missed. I can't say that I would miss him, which was a bit sad as he was my father. But after what he had done to me and my brothers and sister and all that he had put Mother through, as far as I was concerned he was no great loss.

On the day of the funeral Dari took over as usual; she sat in the front pew and I sat behind Mother. I put my hand on

Mother's shoulder to comfort her and Dari told me to leave her alone – *who does she think she is!*

I snapped back that she was my mother too. Dari said nothing, but I had no doubt I wouldn't hear the end of that when we got home. My eldest brother was back from his holiday by this point and at the funeral neither of us were happy with the way Dari was running things. We didn't think that she was doing Mother any good. We all knew she was dying, but Dari wouldn't even let us talk to her about anything at all. She said that Mother wasn't to be bothered by anyone, but Mother would chat to me when Dari had to go home for anything. The trouble was Dari didn't go home very often, in fact it became less and less. She would get our younger brother to go for anything she wanted after he came in from work. The only time the two younger brothers would see Mother was when they came in later on in the evening. Then the three of them would stay up all night drinking beer and joking around as they got more inebriated. I didn't think it was right and neither did my elder brother David. We had a good talk and we decided to have a talk to our doctor to see if there was anything he could do about the situation. Thankfully, he agreed with us and had noticed how Dari was with Mother. He didn't think it was healthy for Mother and said he could put her in hospital if that's what we wanted. We both decided that Mother would be better off there, at least we would be able to see her without Dari interfering and she wouldn't be just sitting there like a zombie. Of course the younger ones weren't very happy with us, they said that we didn't care what Mother wanted and we just wanted her out of the way so we could loot the house. What a load of rubbish. I don't know where they came up with that one, I didn't want to even think about what my parents had, in fact they didn't have anything of value or a lot of money anyway. But that's the way their minds worked.

After that they made sure that we couldn't get in the house. I went round one day to see if my father's little dog wanted to come for a walk with mine, only to find that they had put a big padlock on the inner door, as they knew that David and I had a key for the door. That was the limit.

I went to see Mother in the hospital and as I walked towards her she was sitting in a chair at the side of the bed talking to the woman in the next bed. She looked just like herself and not as if she was dying at all, in fact she looked better there then she did at home. I was so glad that we had taken her into hospital. She asked after Christopher and Dee and seemed more like herself, taking an interest in things again. I didn't tell her about what the others had done with the house or how we had all fallen out, it didn't seem right to tell her anything like that. You know, even then she still managed to make me feel unwanted.

In the end all she could go on about was how good Dari was, in coming home to look after her. She had no praise for me going out to get her nice things to eat or magazines to read or taking cooked meals down for both her and my father. I didn't have the money to do these things as I had taken time off work to look after them both, but I did it. Yet it was all, 'Dari, Mike and Edward do this…' – nothing changes, does it? My last words to my mother were, 'You never ever loved me anyway.' And to that I got no response.

Dari, Mike and Edward took her out of hospital and moved her back home and there was nothing anyone could do. I never saw her again; it wasn't worth the hassle of battling with my sister to get access. David tried a number of times, but they kept the lock on the door even when they were in. About a week later Mother died and my younger brother came round to inform me and also to give me a warning that if I said anything out of place at the funeral I would get beaten up by the rest of my family. I went to see Mother at the funeral parlour with Dee, but I kept Christopher out of it and told him he should remember his gran as she had been. It wasn't her in the box anyway; when I stroked her face it just felt like wax. I can't say what emotions I was feeling, I wasn't devastated as most daughters would be; it was more like a great big weight had been lifted. There would be no more waiting for approval, no more running around after her hoping that she would give a bit of praise and not just run me down all the time.

I loved my mother beyond reason when I think of it now; she died having never given me anything. I will never ever know why she treated me as she did. A friend of mine seems to think that it had something to do with the fact that my twin died and that perhaps Mother blamed me for her death. What can I say except that I had always felt a part of me missing too, and Mother should have thought about my feelings as regards my twin. It was never talked about, I only know I had a twin at all because, on the rare times my parents did talk, Father would say they had thrown the best one away in the bucket and were stuck with me. I know he said it in jest, but it still hurt and made me wonder what it would have been like if my twin had lived.

Dee and Christopher went to Mother's funeral in my place ,as I wasn't sure that I wouldn't say something to the younger members of the family. I had said my goodbyes in the funeral parlour, and was fine with that.

XX

After the funeral Dee told me that each of my siblings had thrown a rose over the coffin, one at a time. My mother had been carried out of the house and an hour later they were back, carrying out the washer and all the things they could get. I never wanted any of those things, but it would have been nice to have some photographs.

Shortly after Mother's death they asked us if we wanted to give some money towards the seat that they were having put in the churchyard in memory of my parents. David and I both said that they had excluded us from our mother while she was living so we didn't think we would partake now that she was dead. Anyway it was only for show. Dari's husband sent a long letter to both David and me saying how we had been bad children and done nothing for our mother in the last days of her life. He only knew what his wife had told him, but what had it to do with him anyway? Nevertheless he hurt me with the things he said. My mother's last days, her funeral and the park bench caused a rift in the family. We didn't speak to each other for three years.

Dari went back to America and had another child three years later and called it Norah after my mother. Her husband left her and is now remarried; I suppose he had enough of being controlled. Edward went home and by the time I next saw him he was down on his luck and suffering from depression. I took him for a night out in a gay club, I thought it would cheer him up and for a moment it did.

Mike threw my elder brother out of the family home where he had lived all his life. Unfortunately, as my parents had allowed Mike to buy it, it was tough luck for David. Mike then went to America for a holiday where he met Dari's husband's niece and spent his time with her while he was there. I don't suppose she knew he had a girl living with him back home in England and he was taking the best from both worlds.

Mike had the nerve to phone Dee and I up one evening about two months after my parents had died, half-cut with the booze, to tell us that his Doberman dog was at the vet's. She had a twisted gut, which wasn't much of a surprise as my mother had been the one who looked after it, and now she'd gone Mike couldn't manage. He wanted us to pick him up and take him to the vet's to say goodbye to his dog, and of course I obliged. Dee was always good in these circumstances, she said that we would pick the dog up and take it home and bury it for him.

As we put the last bit of dirt over the dog, Mike came running out off the house threatening to hit us with the shovel and ranting and raving about how we had robbed him.

He eventually married the American girl and she came to England against her parents' wishes. He married her so that he could go and live in America. Years later he turned up again on my doorstep with a pregnant wife and not the American one, another one he had married. Out of them all I suppose Mike was the worst.

He had turned into an alcoholic; Dari had done him no favours, she had managed all his money and treated him as a child with an allowance. Thankfully, he eventually returned to America. It's not that I didn't love him as I did, I just couldn't help him. The last I heard is that he had been in a clinic and dried out; his fourth wife – the mother of his son – had died at the age of only twenty, so he had his son to bring up on his own. Another generation to feel sorry for.

All my brothers and sister apart from Fred were down on their luck, no good had come out of their greed when my parents died. The opportunity arose for Dee to start a small business, a trade stand at dog shows; she was in a position to put in some of the money towards it herself and I was going to make up the difference. I told to go for it. She was worried that she would not be able to manage the paperwork so I suggested that I take on that side of the business. I thought that if she had another interest of her own, then things might get better between us. All we seemed to do in those days was argue and it got to the point where we weren't even sharing the same bed as I slept downstairs.

A small amount of stock was included in the purchase, as well as some stands and tables. I wrote letters and contacted dog show secretaries to arrange bookings and the ball started rolling. Eventually we had to buy more stock and a van to transport everything to and from the shows, so I took out a bank loan. The whole venture took off and we found we had so many bookings that I had to become more involved. In order to make it work we had to split the workload and I took over all the office duties while Dee went out to the shows. Dee did not seem to be able to manage doing a show on her own and persuaded our next-door neighbour to go along with her.

It ended up feeling like I was doing all the work – booking, sorting out stock and re-ordering – and for little rewards. At this point the relationship took a bit of a tumble and, after thirteen years during which Dee continued to take off whenever it suited her, I felt I had reached the end of the road. One night we had a big argument and I asked her to leave.

I think I had just sailed along with the relationship because I didn't like being on my own. By the end of it, all we seemed to do was argue and I was working myself into the ground ordering, packing and booking the shows and I couldn't do it any more. Worst of all there was no love between us; we hadn't made love in longer than I could remember, Dee would always say she wasn't in the mood. I asked her on several occasions to see the doctor about it, but it didn't seem as important to her as it was to me. Perhaps I had been associating making love with love itself.

I went to the gay club quite a lot after Dee left. Searching once again to love or be loved. I did meet someone at the club, but try as I may I couldn't make it work. All she seemed to want to do when we saw each other was stay in bed. Me on the other hand, I've always felt that I needed the sexual part, but wanted someone that I could go out with and share my life with. Sometimes I think I'm asking too much but then I think, surely it's not too much to ask to be loved and cared about, is it?

My son, Christopher, went off to Salford to train as a nurse. He started out caring for old people in a home when he left school and was very good at it. As regards him caring for me, well I don't know. He could sometimes seem to be very selfish to me, though I suppose that much is my fault. I gave him everything as he grew up, as much love as I knew how as I never wanted him to feel unloved. I thought that I had to make it up to him for the lack of a father. I know now that it isn't so, so all you out there don't make that mistake and give your all, as one day it will be thrown back.

Christopher failed at nursing and his love life was whiled away. He returned to me, bringing with him a drink problem, and carried on like that most of the way through his life. Sometimes he was OK with me, but most of the time I didn't think he really cared about anyone. Anyone who has been or known an alcoholic will know what I am talking about, they will do anything just to get a drink and don't stop to think who they hurt on the way.

Christopher has turned out OK in the end though and that's all that matters. He no longer drinks and often tells me how much he loves me. He's still selfish in a lot of ways, but when he meets the right person I hope he will be OK. That's all one can do really, hope for the best.

Well I could ramble on and on telling you about all the things that have gone on in my life, but I won't. All I can say now is that I don't think I turned into such a bad person through it all, or at least so my friends say. All my life I have searched for love and acceptance yet never felt secure. I always thought that if I was treated nicely then it was because someone wanted something from me, never because they really liked who I was. Mother often said I was no good to anyone, that I couldn't do anything right. I never looked right no matter how I dressed, and I still don't have any confidence, even now; it's so nice when you get told you look nice. I will still do almost anything for anyone as I need to feel needed. And you know, these feelings will be with me for the rest of my life all because of Mother.

The bright side is that I have a house and a car, but most of all my lovely dogs who I know love me as much as I love them.

Printed in the United Kingdom
by Lightning Source UK Ltd.
117521UKS00001B/15